In the Studio, a new series from Hauser & Wirth Publishers, gives readers a behind-the-scenes view of artists at work. Each book focuses on a major figure of twentieth- or twenty-first-century art, offering an introduction to their influences, materials, and techniques. Written by leading scholars and critics and generously illustrated, *In the Studio* titles are the perfect companion for longstanding art lovers and newcomers alike.

The first volume in the series explores the life and work of Phyllida Barlow; forthcoming books focus on Lee Lozano and Louise Bourgeois.

Yinka Elujoba is a Nigerian writer and art critic.
He contributes regularly to the *New York Times* arts
section and has been published in several magazines
and journals. He holds an MFA in Art Criticism and Writing
from the School of Visual Arts, New York. He was awarded
the Rabkin Prize in 2021 and the Andy Warhol Foundation
Arts Writers Grant in 2023.

Jack Whitten

Yinka
Elujoba

Hauser & Wirth Publishers

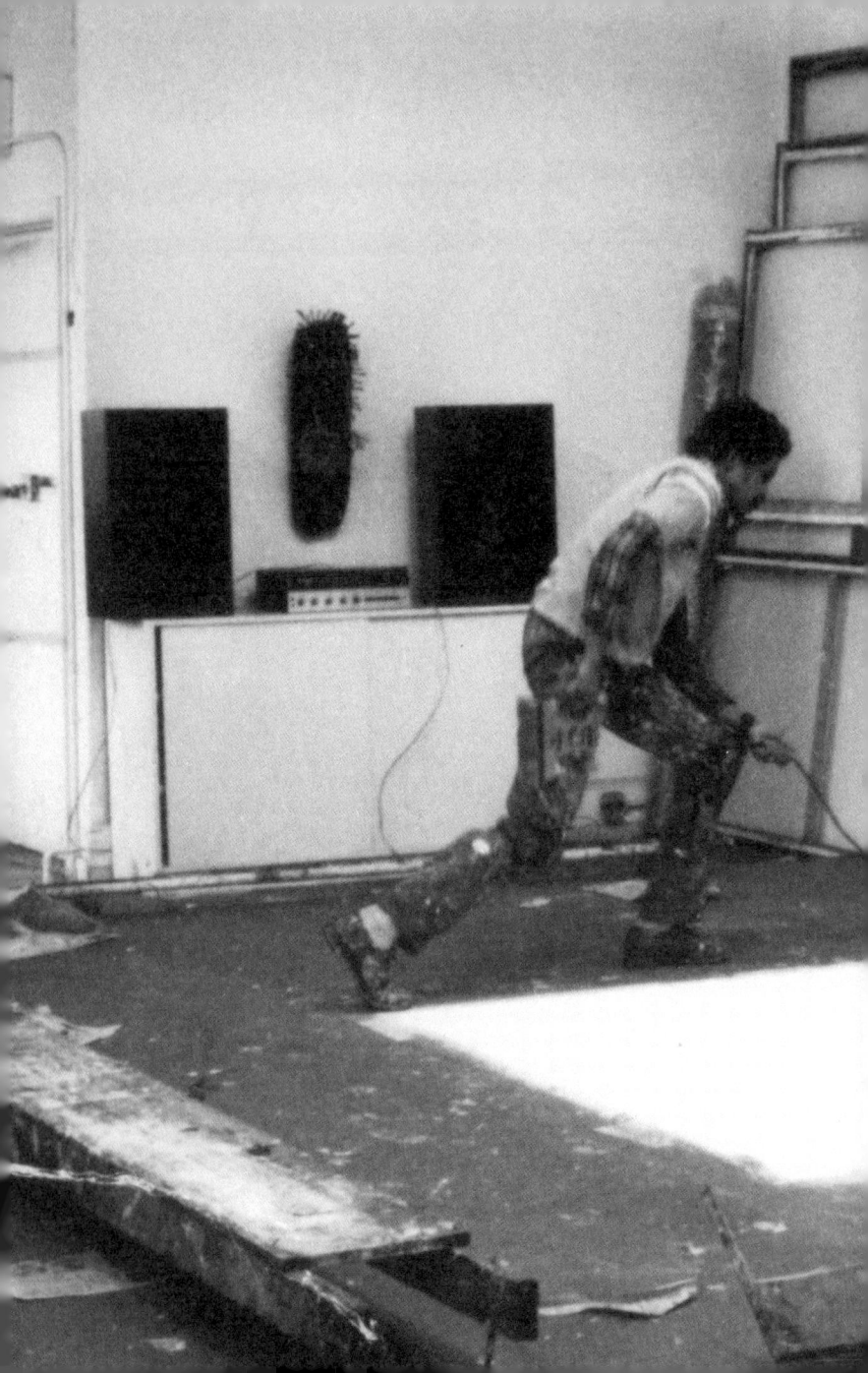

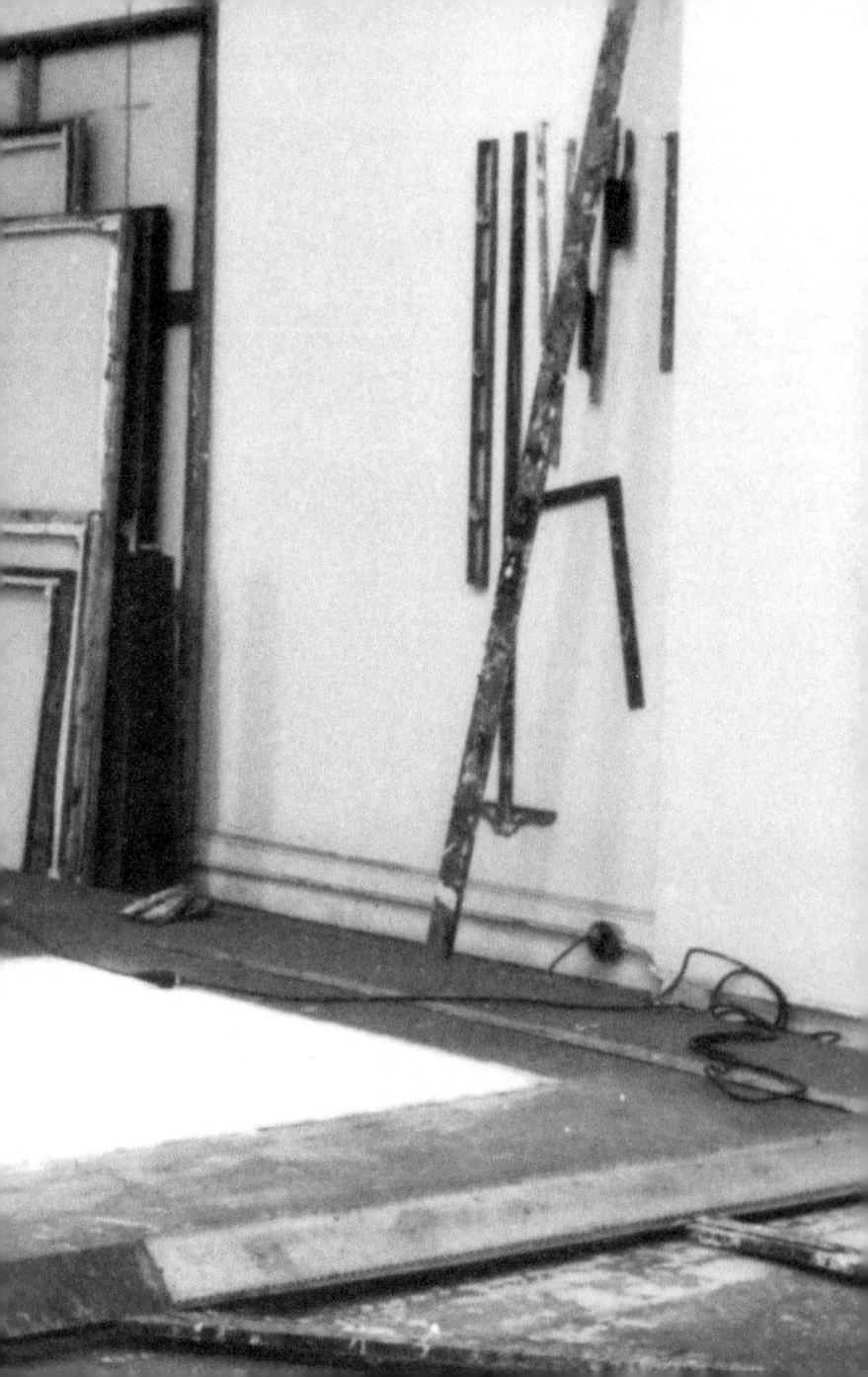

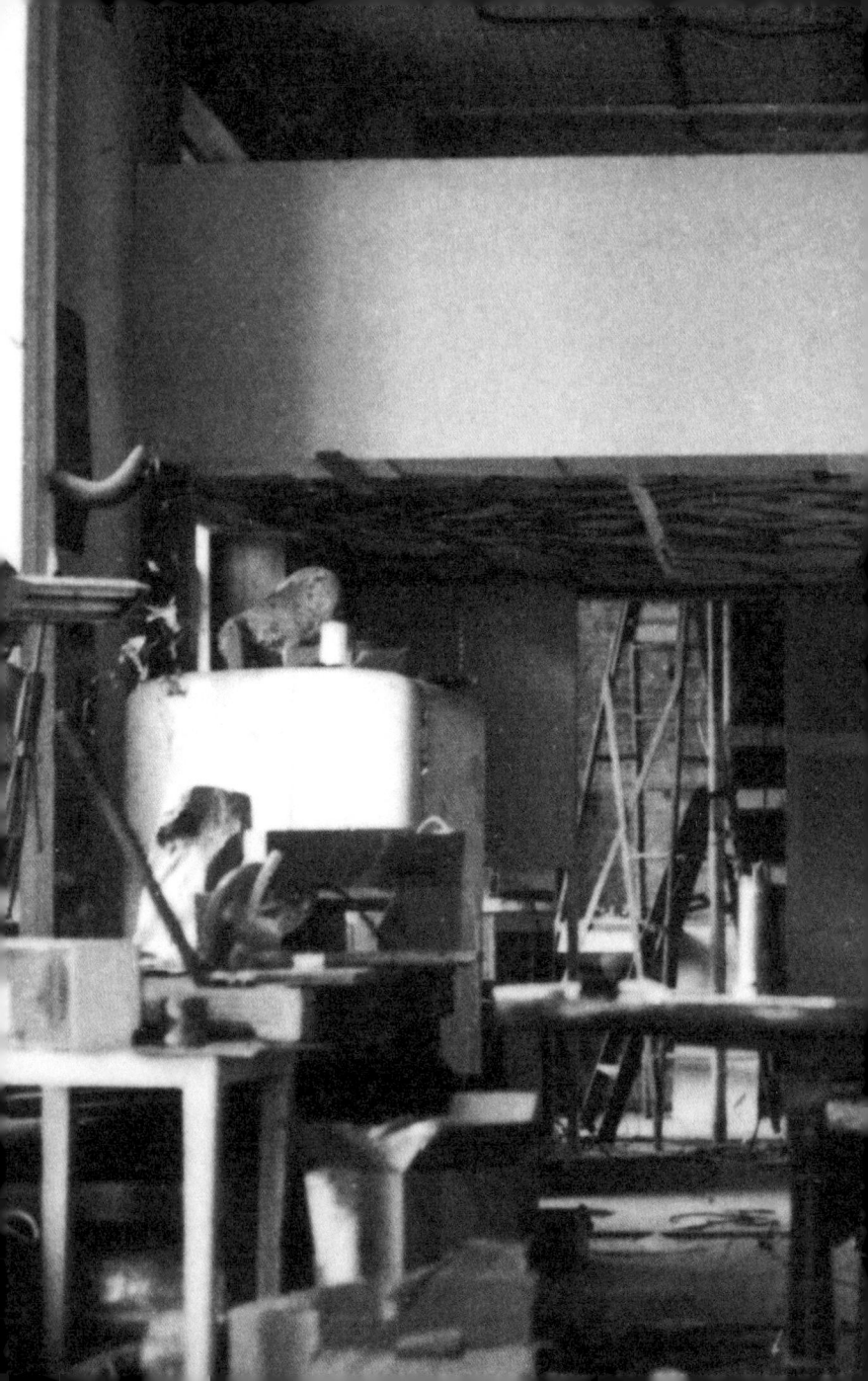

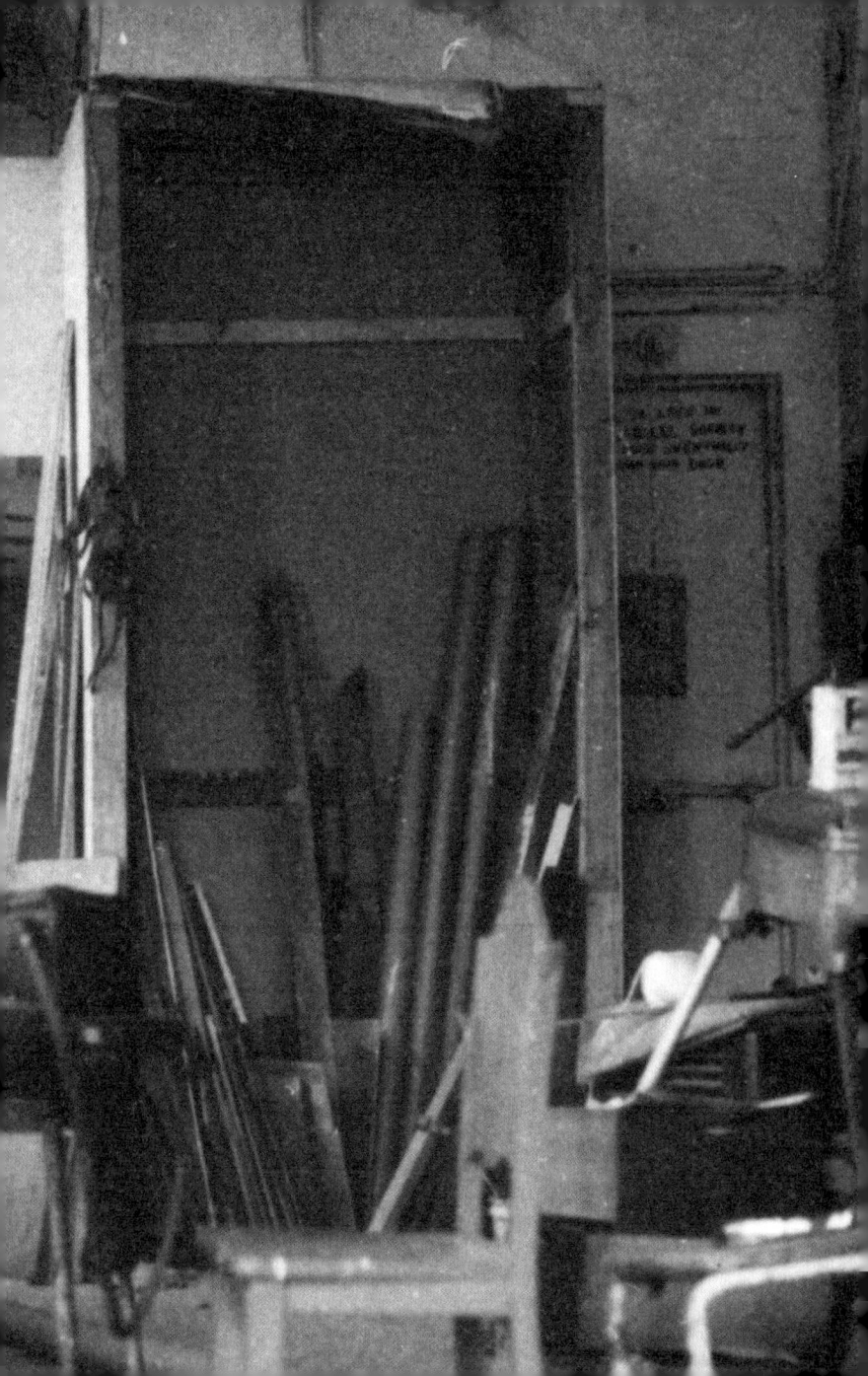

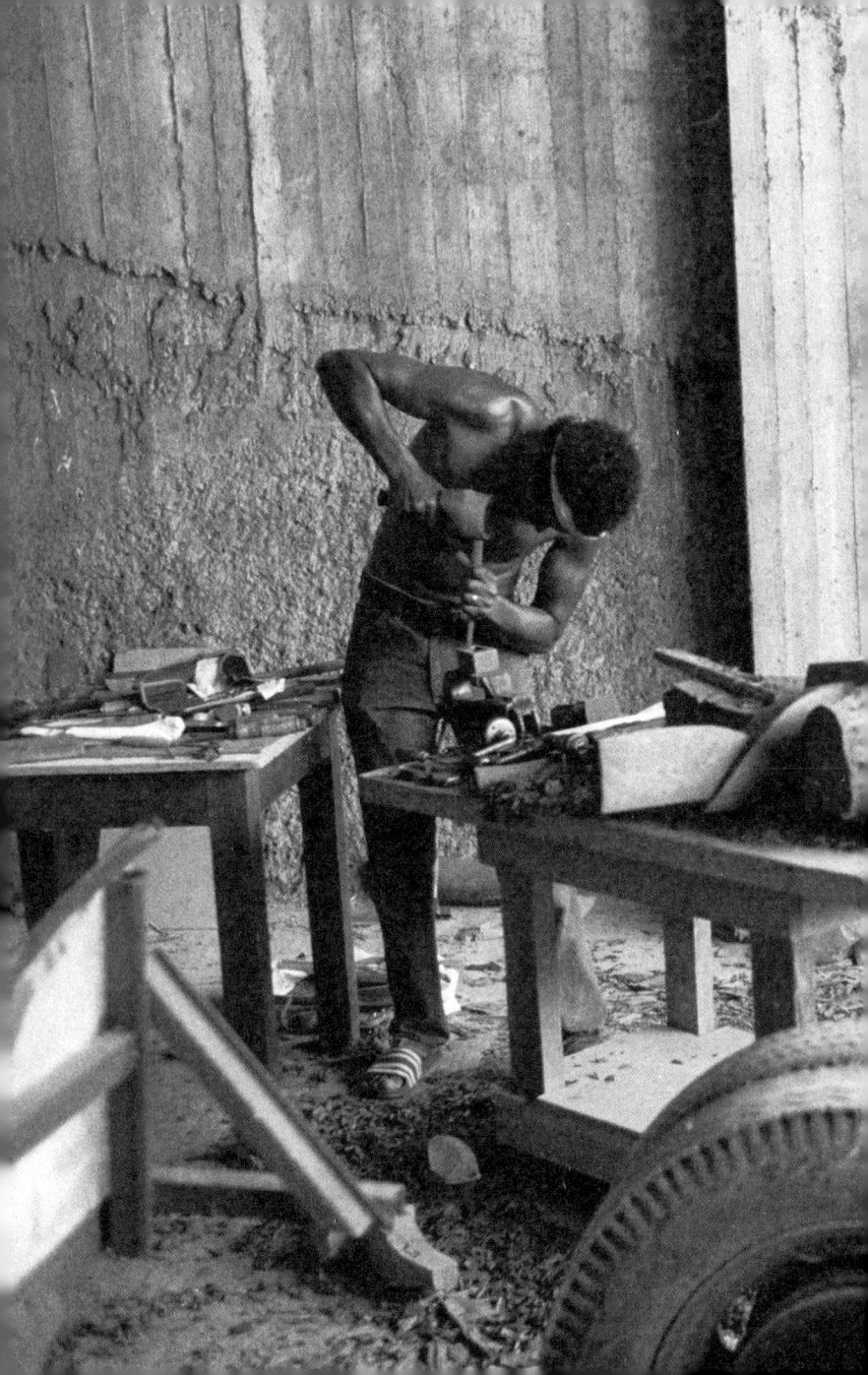

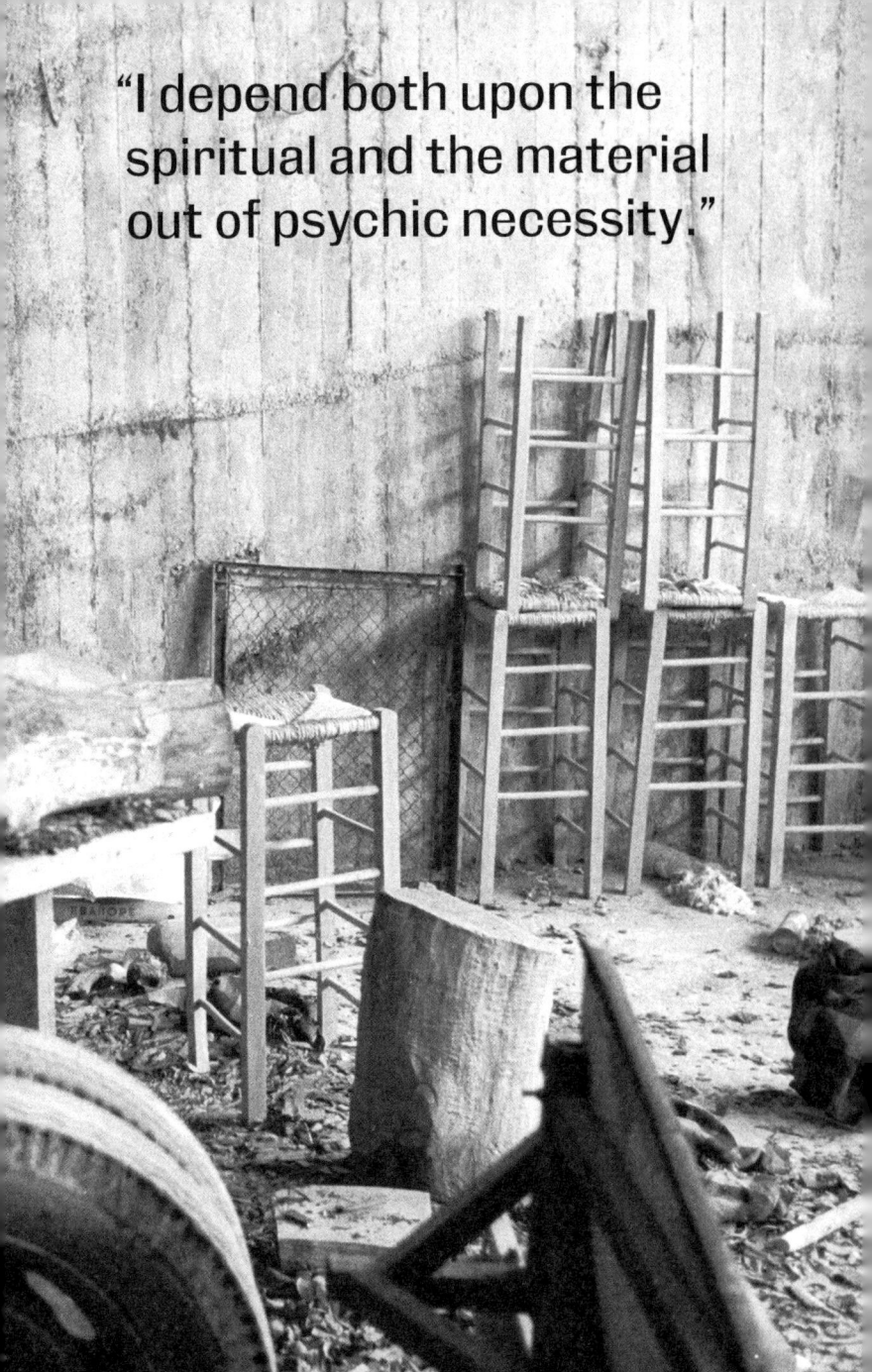

"I depend both upon the spiritual and the material out of psychic necessity."

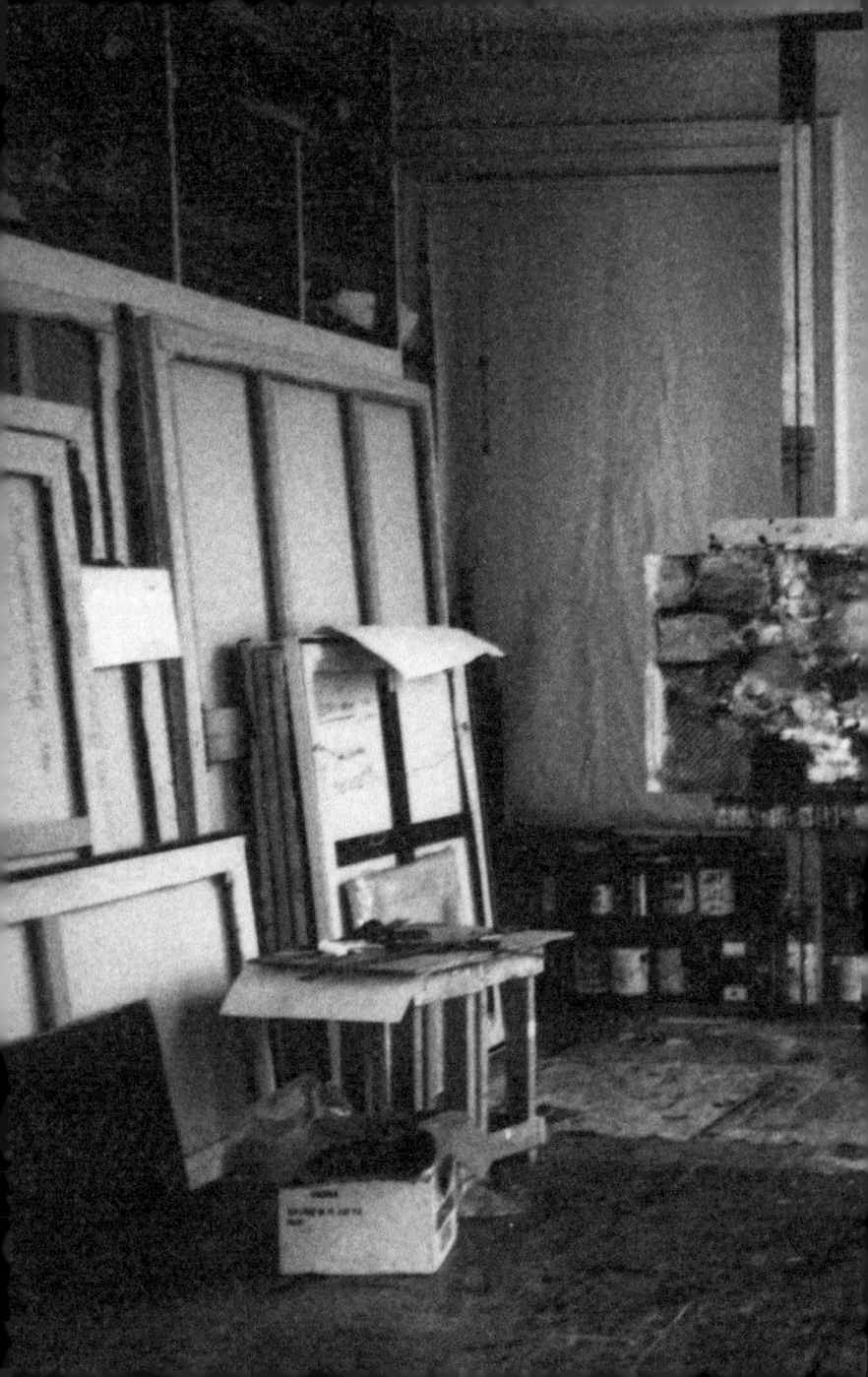

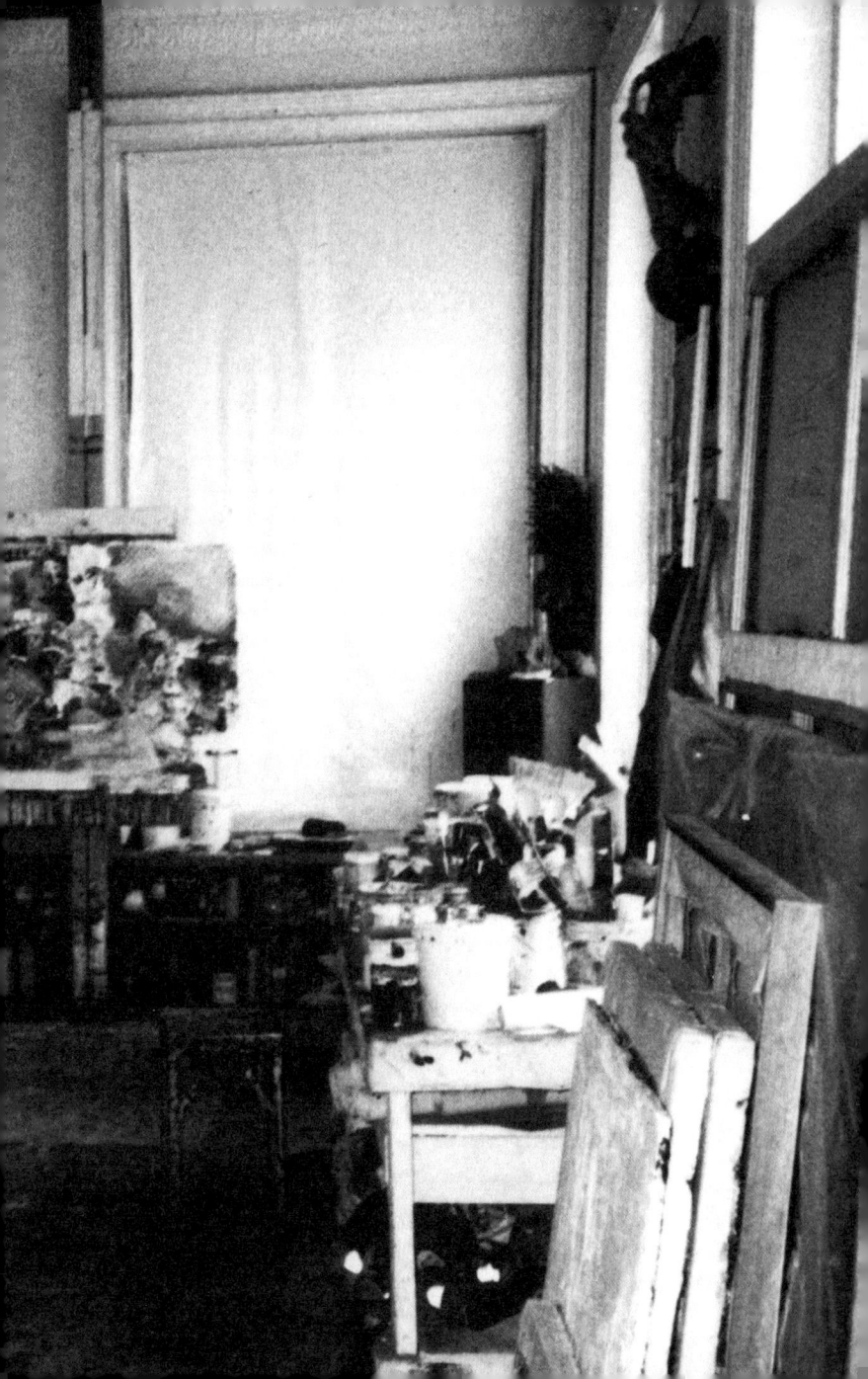

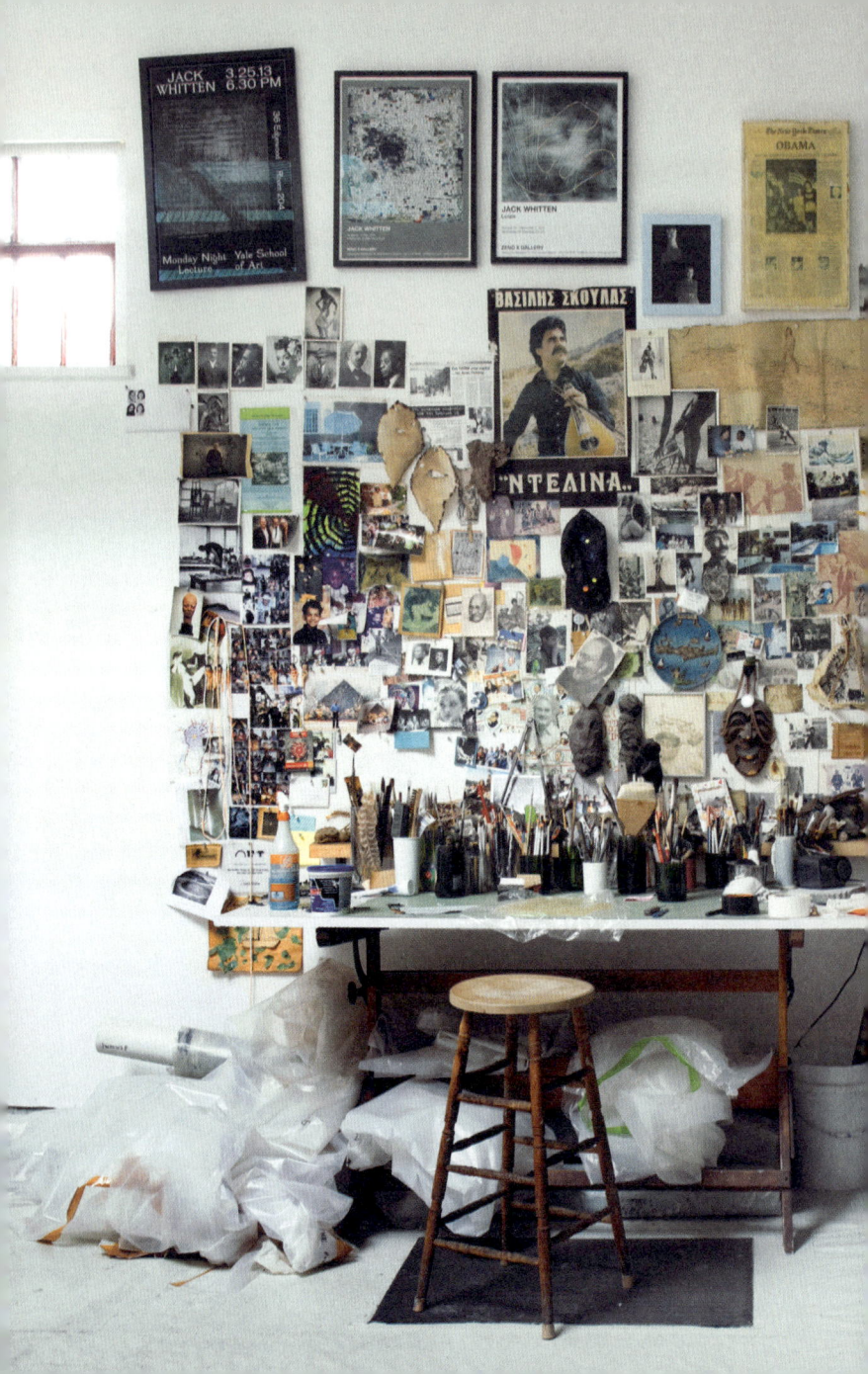

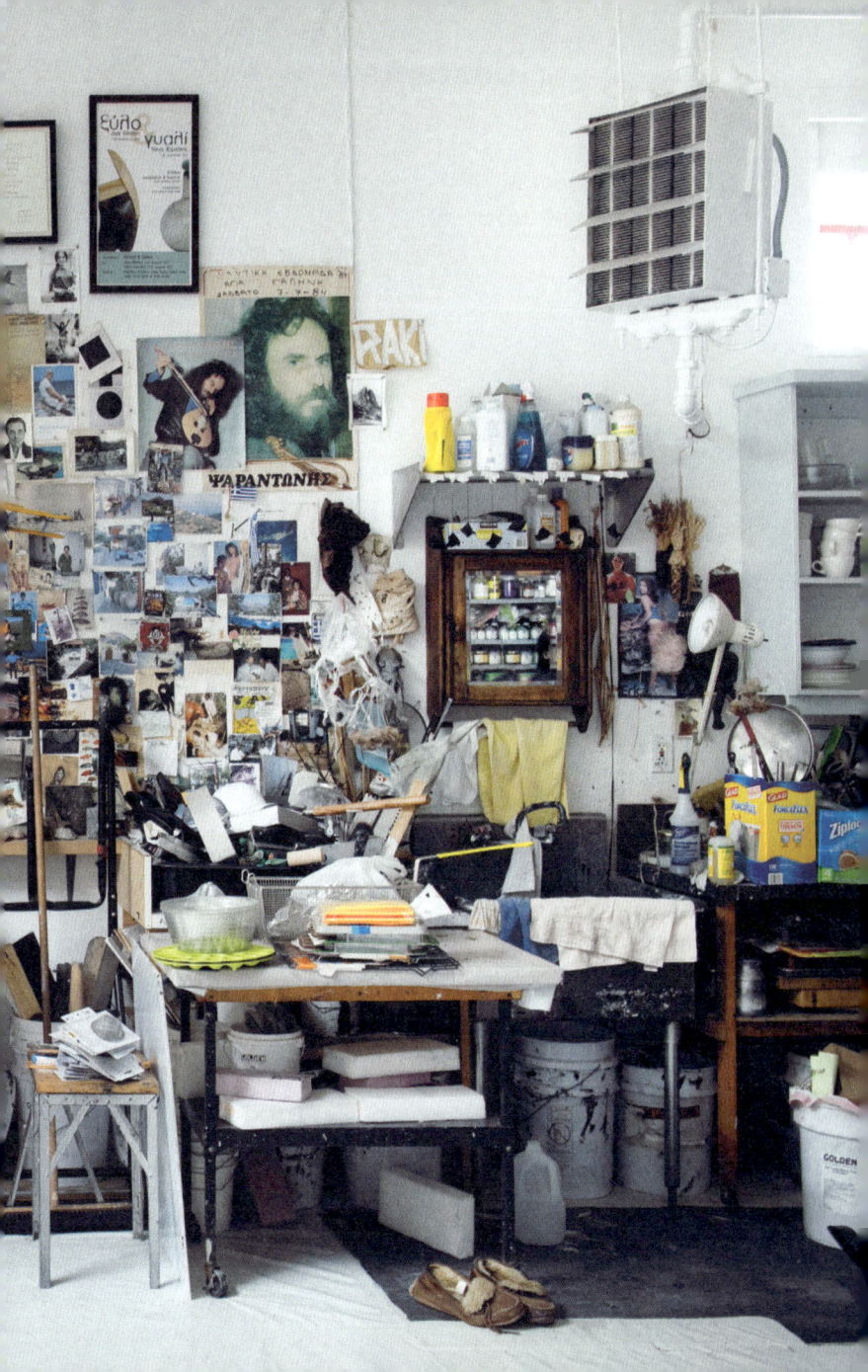

Contents

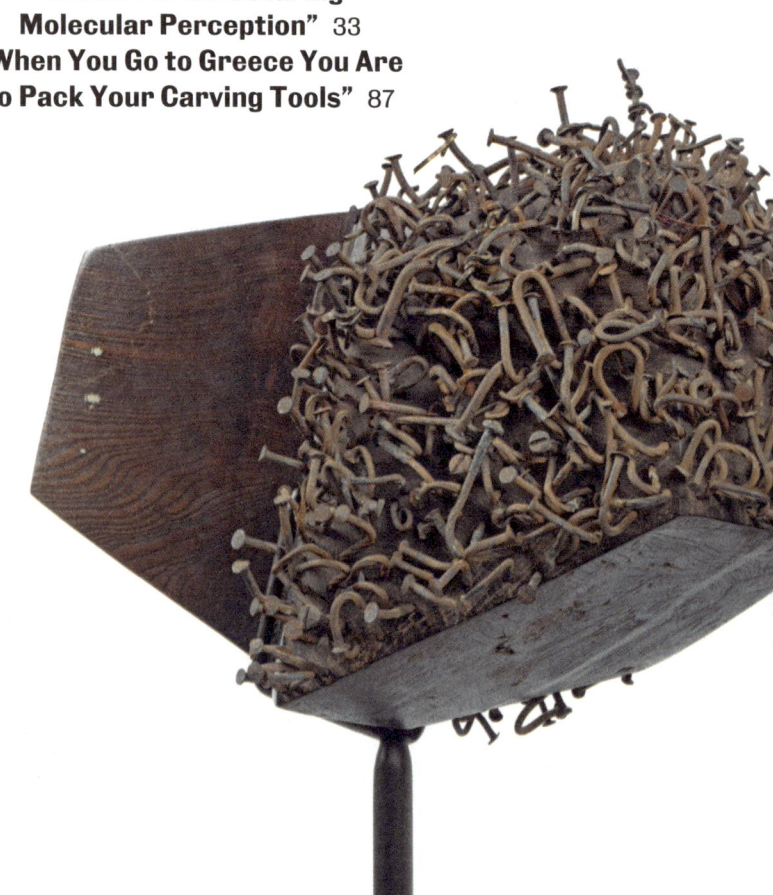

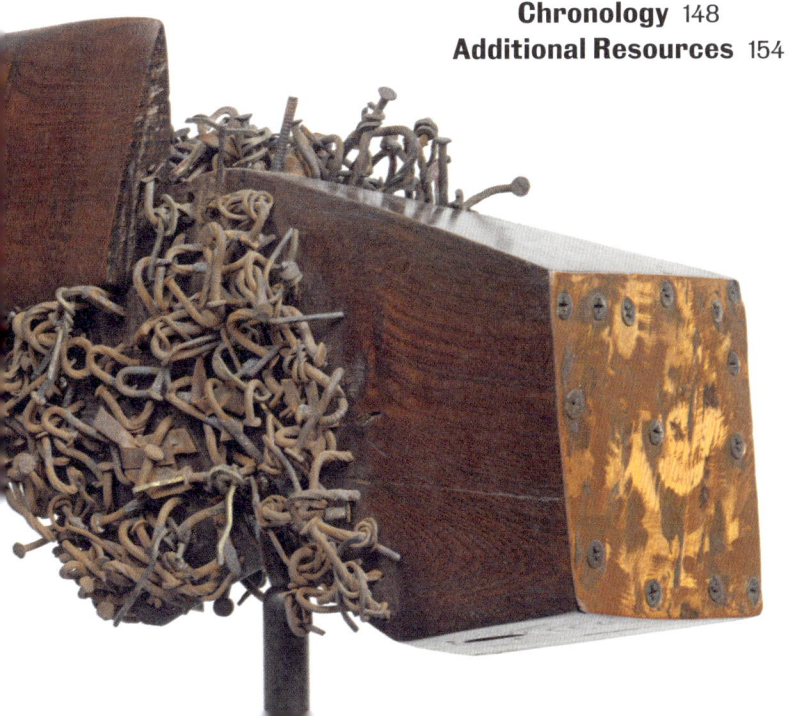

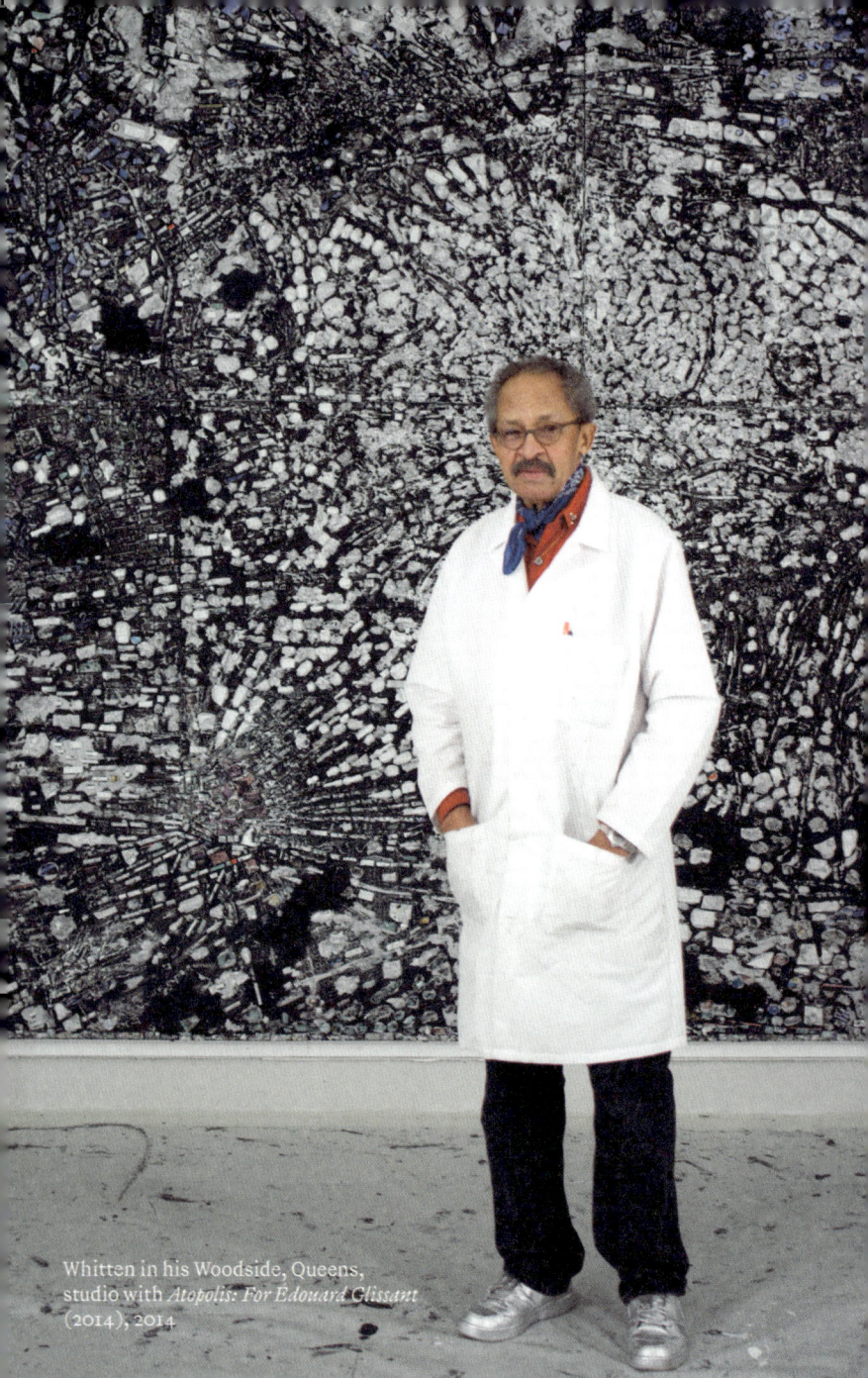

Whitten in his Woodside, Queens,
studio with *Atopolis: For Édouard Glissant*
(2014), 2014

A Love of Process

The greatness of an artist is perhaps proportionate
to how much they push the limits of the form in which
they work. Think of what Caravaggio did with tenebrism,
or Picasso with Cubism. Jack Whitten can be said to have
done something similar with abstraction, contributing
an approach that questioned, played with, and expanded
the materiality of paint itself.

Starting out in the 1960s, Whitten sought a global
aesthetic, something that connected his work with
the visual vocabulary of other cultures. Deeply interested
in inventing the future of painting, he loved the process as
much as the outcome. He put his craftsmanship skills to use,
creating custom tools for manipulating paint that helped
him develop new ways of making canvases that advanced
beyond the prevailing methods of his time, escaping the
long shadows cast by Abstract Expressionists like Willem
de Kooning and Barnett Newman. Pulling from inspirations
as varied as jazz and quantum physics, Whitten was tireless
in his experimentation.

Whitten was also a sculptor, practicing for the most part
in Greece, where he made a second home in the small town
of Agia Galini on the island of Crete. He fused his interests
in different cultures—African modes of carving, Greek island
life and mythology—in his sculptures, imbuing them with
a life-giving spirituality.

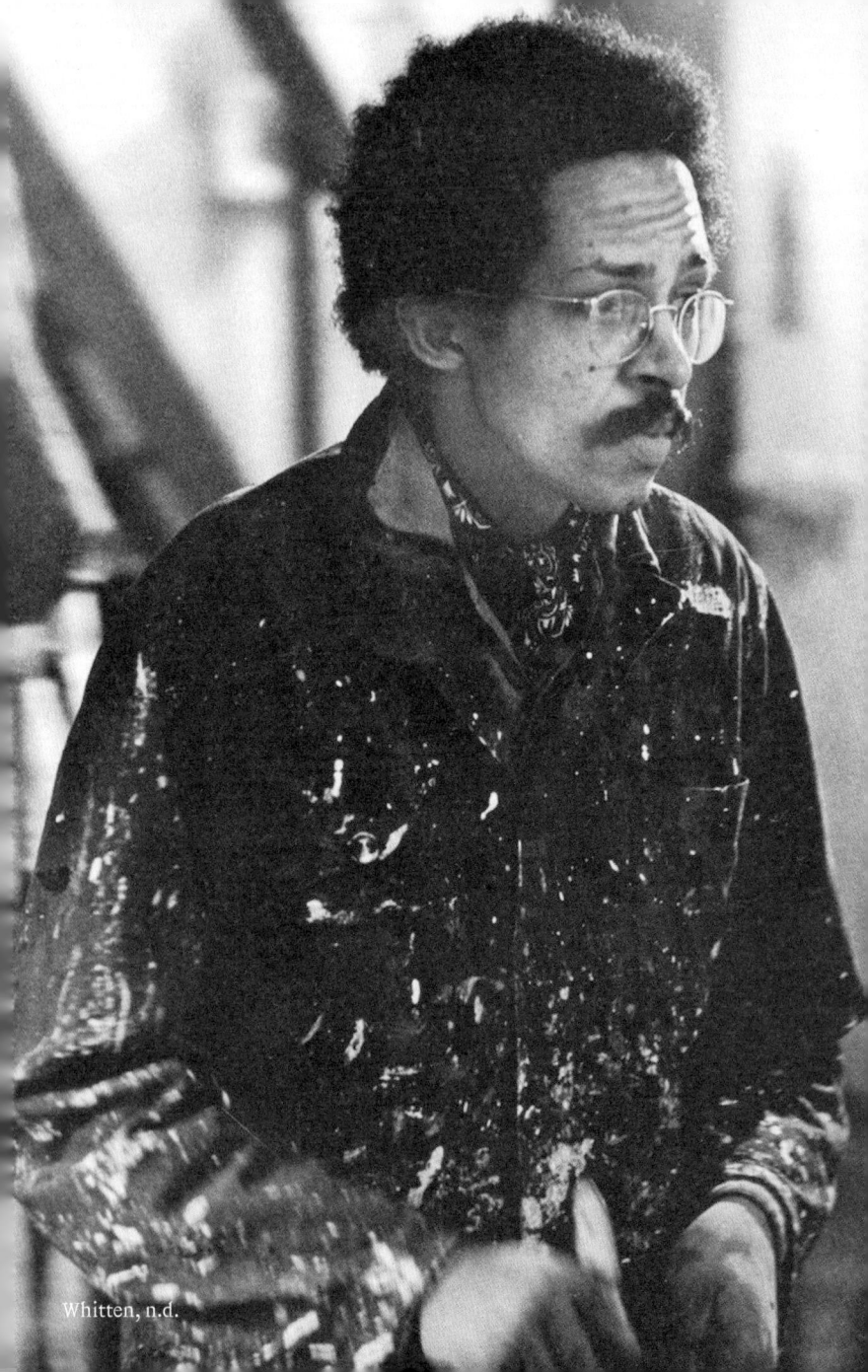
Whitten, n.d.

Subjective Images

In the 1960s, when he began to seriously rethink his approach to painting, Whitten realized that although his focus was abstraction, he had been subconsciously obsessed with producing what he later described as "subjective images." These subjective images, he recognized, were human faces, and he saw them everywhere: on the beach when he stumbled on a pebble, in a pan when he cooked, in every cloud that moved in the sky above his head.

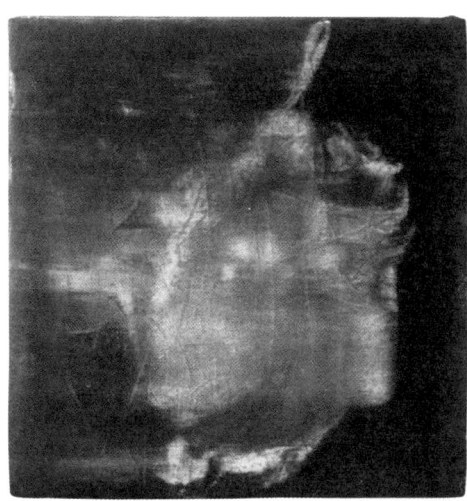

Head IV Lynching, 1964.
Acrylic on styrofoam
cloth mounted on board,
$11\frac{1}{8} \times 11\frac{1}{8}$ in. (28.3 × 28.3 cm)

This was the era when, around the world, countries were breaking free of colonial grips, moving into independence, and redefining their national identities. The United States, too, was boiling, with the civil rights movement at home and the Vietnam War abroad making for one of the country's most defining political moments. There were awakenings of all sorts, including among intellectuals and artists. Reflecting on this period almost a decade later,

Whitten recalled, "I realized that this was the beginning of the development of a new esthetic[,] one that develops out of my search for identity[,] out of my particular unique sensibility."

Whitten had long noticed that his mind worked better (especially in painting) when he made associations between seemingly disparate sources. He was passionate about jazz (pp. 117–24), with its improvisatory nature requiring innovation at every turn. Science and technology showed him new possibilities, as well: the uncanny field of fractal geometry and its nesting of successively smaller copies of a pattern within each other helped him focus the reflection of light into his painting through his use of tesserae (pp. 33–51). He also recognized how inventions in engineering were reshaping mechanical and electronic imaging and he wanted his painting to visualize that new perception of the modern world.

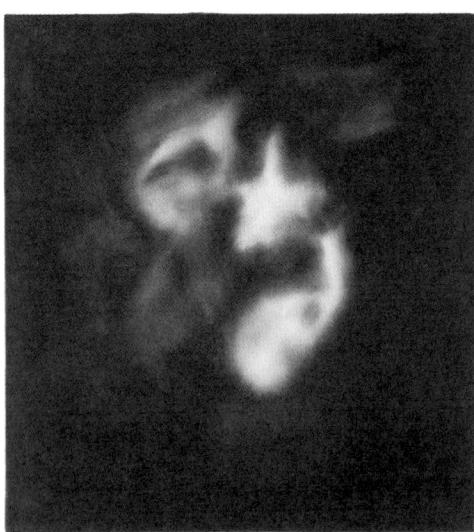

Psychic Eclipse, 1964.
Nylon fabric and acrylic on canvas, $26\frac{1}{8} \times 24\frac{7}{8}$ in. (66.4×63.2 cm)

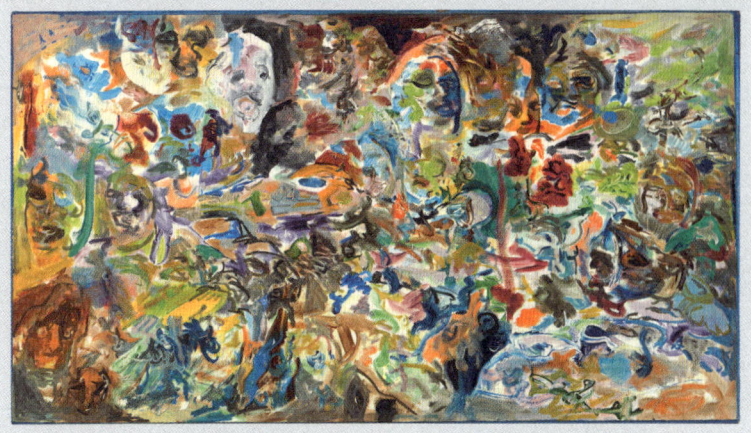

Garden in Bessemer VI, 1968
Oil on canvas, 43 × 79¼ in. (109.2 × 201.3 cm)

Whitten had various ongoing questions he sought
to answer as he worked, above all how he could escape
what he called "touch," his term for painterly gestures
inherited from European art. One of his last works
employing touch was *Garden in Bessemer VI*, its rough
mesh of swabs still resembling the expressive marks in
paintings by de Kooning and Norman Lewis. Whitten's goal
was to break free of such defaults, and perhaps create
a new way of seeing in the process.

   Whitten was dissatisfied with the expressive character
of the abstract canvases being made around him when
he first began painting; they seemed to him monotonous
and repetitive and disrespectful of the essence of paint
as a material in and of itself. In January 1973, he wrote
in his notes, "I see no paintings to excite me. I must look
at my surroundings for purity for honesty for absolute
materialization of matter; it is not to be found in the
painting of today's art world. On the sidewalk I can see
more purity of form than in any New York art gallery."

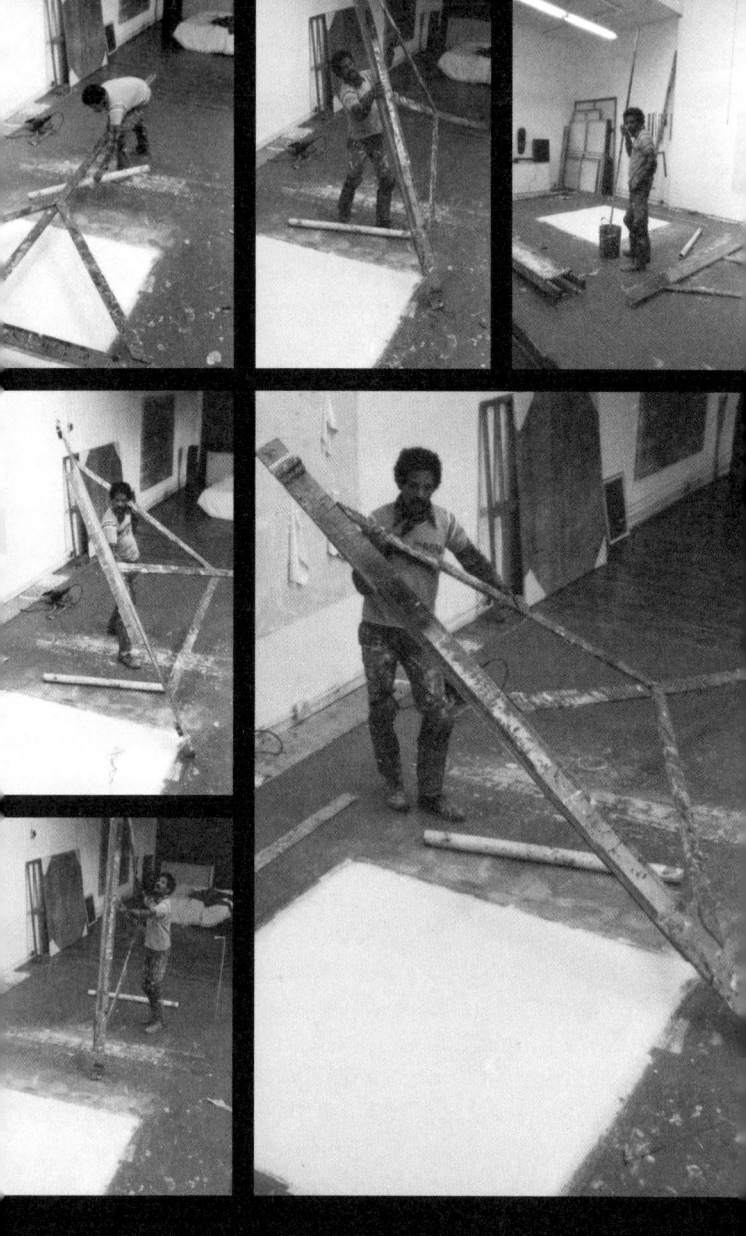

Whitten using one of his developers in his Crosby Street studio, ca. 1974–75.

"I Just Want a Slab of Paint"

Whitten made many of his painting tools himself. He had long experimented with the surfaces of his canvases, adding and removing paint, seeking patterns that would allow the material to come alive. In the early 1970s he began working with a special set of rakes or, as he called them, developers, that he constructed from heavy wood bases and comblike teeth of varying thicknesses.

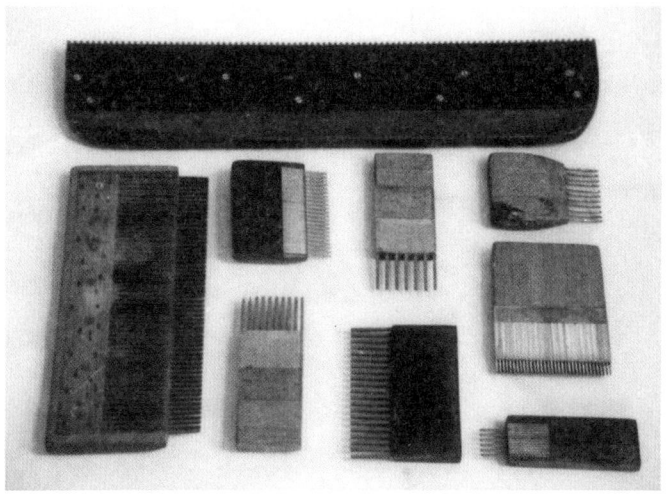

Whitten's smaller developers, in a photograph by the artist, 1983

In 1972, of his tireless search for processes that could effect the results he sought, he wrote: "I've done so much. I've tried everything.... I've made all sort of formal announcements about the importance of space, volumentric surface.... Space is important: that much is true. I still come back to surface. Please I am trying hard not to be confused. This shit is complicated! To be as clear as possible without getting confused. I JUST WANT A SLAB of PAINT."

Thereafter he began experimenting with making what he referred to as "slab" paintings, in which he would meticulously layer thick coats of acrylic paint on a canvas laid on the floor, then drag the developer along the surface while the acrylic was still wet. "I wanted this slab to be a concrete fact without any psychological meaning," he reflected on these works in an unpublished text from 2014. "Non-relational thinking was the key: a single pull with the developer reduced the picture plane to a single gesture."

It was with this approach that he made many of his signature paintings, including *Clearview II* (1970), *Golden Space* (1971), *Zulu Tea Parlor* (1973), *April's Shark* (1974), *Delacroix's Palette* (1974), and *The Speedchaser* (1975).

Golden Spaces, 1971. Acrylic on canvas, 76 × 103 in. (193 × 261.6 cm)

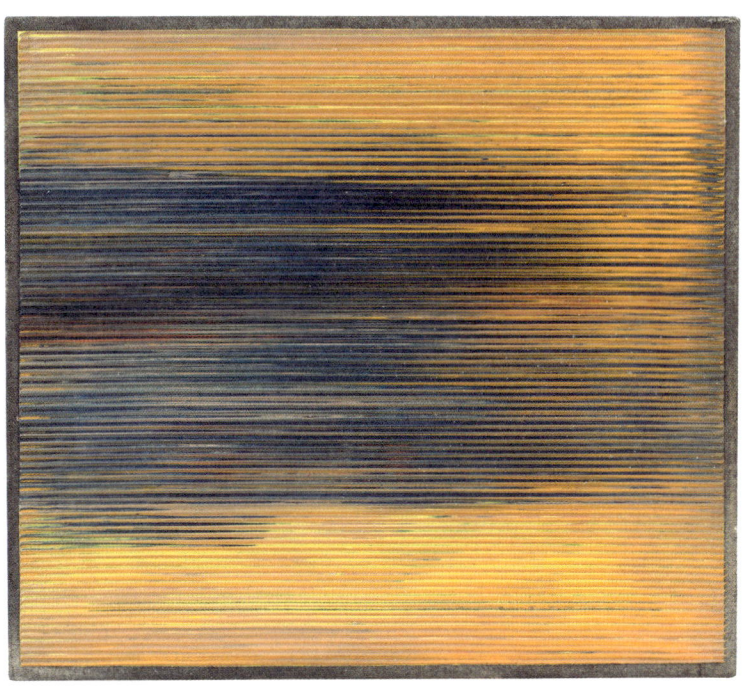

Clearview II, 1970. Acrylic on canvas, 14 × 16 in. (35.6 × 40.6 cm)

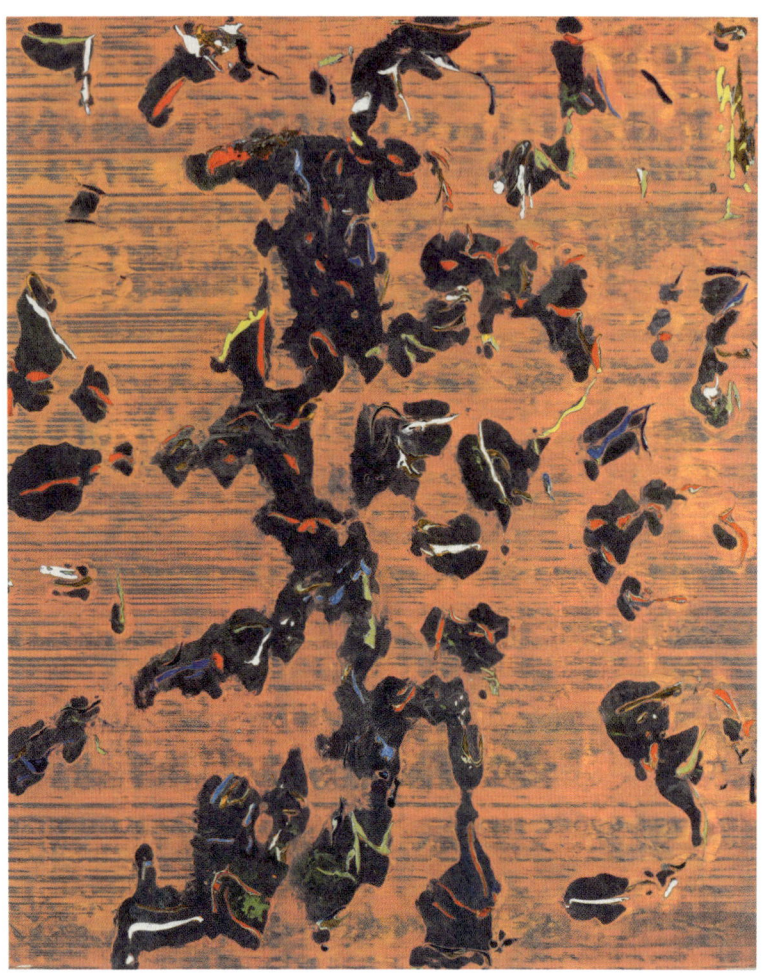

Zulu Tea Parlor, 1973. Acrylic on canvas, 71½ × 60 in. (181.6 × 152.4 cm)

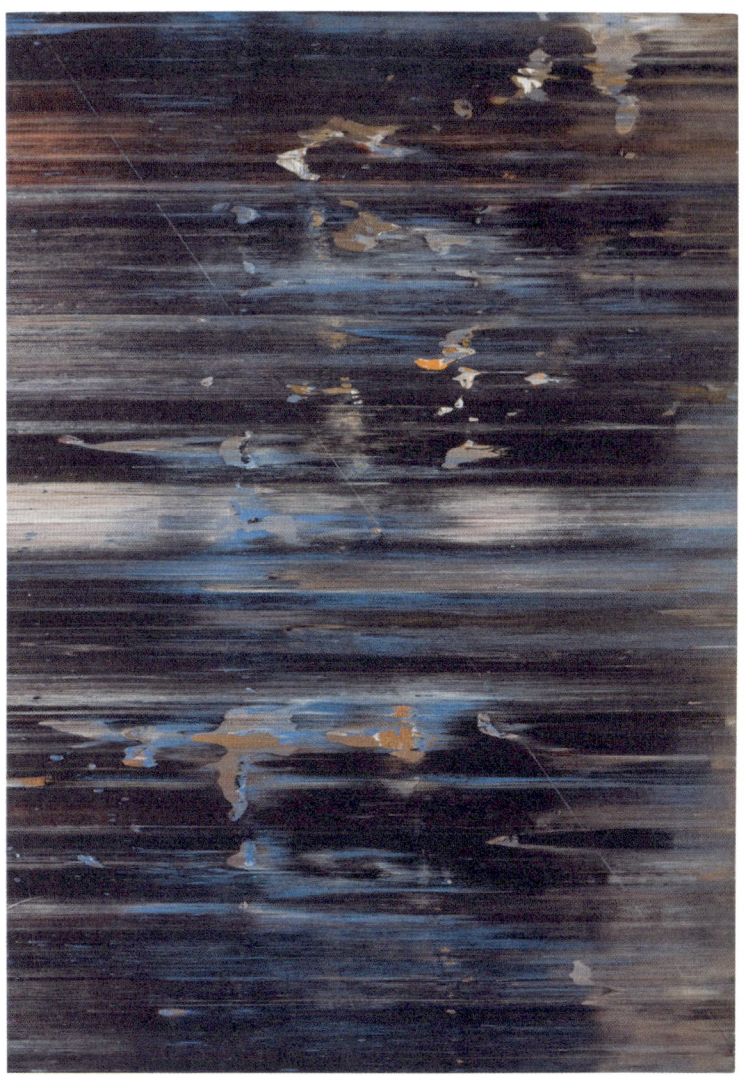

April's Shark, 1974. Acrylic on canvas, 73¼ × 53 in. (186.1 × 134.6 cm).
Detail, pp. 28–29

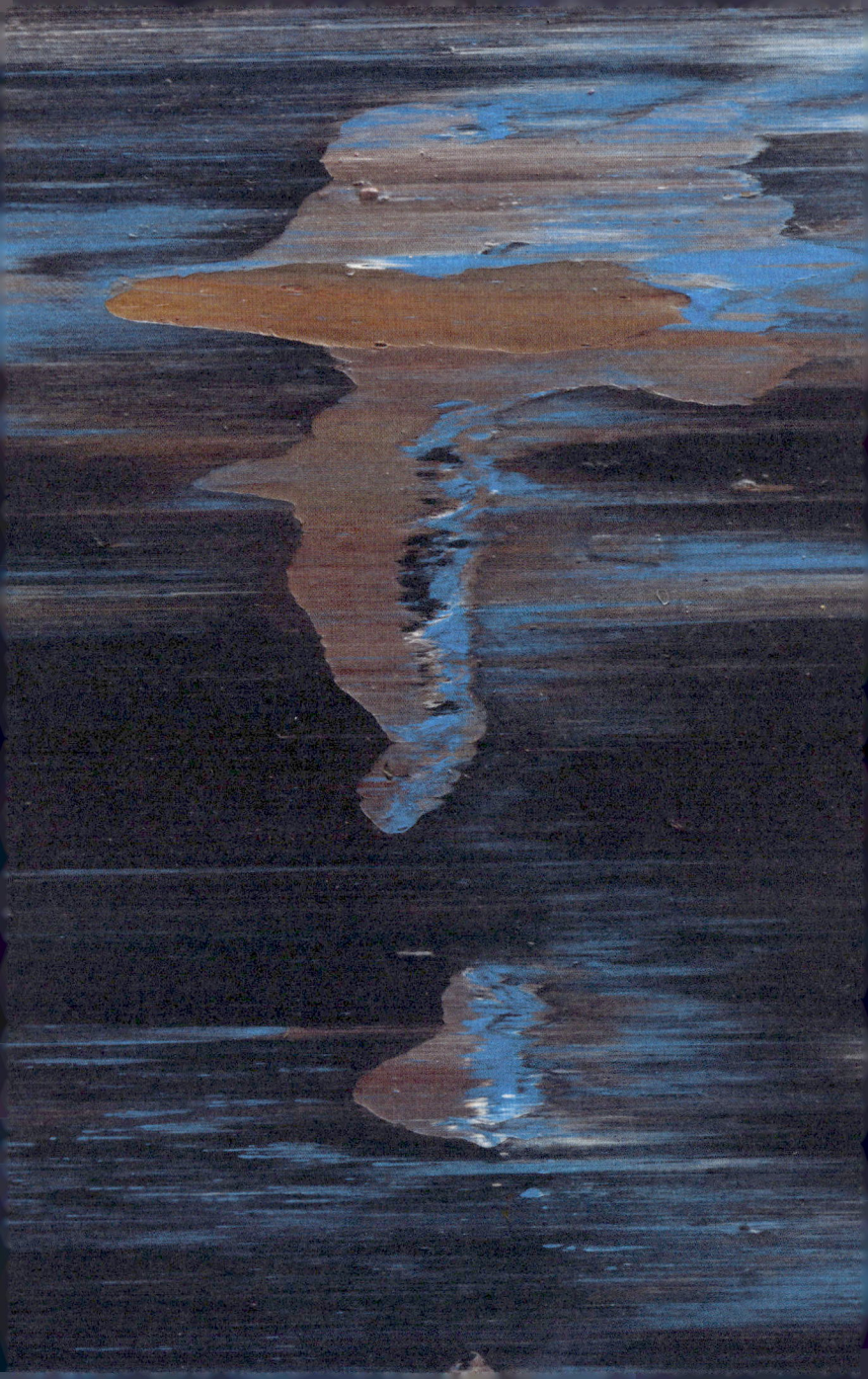

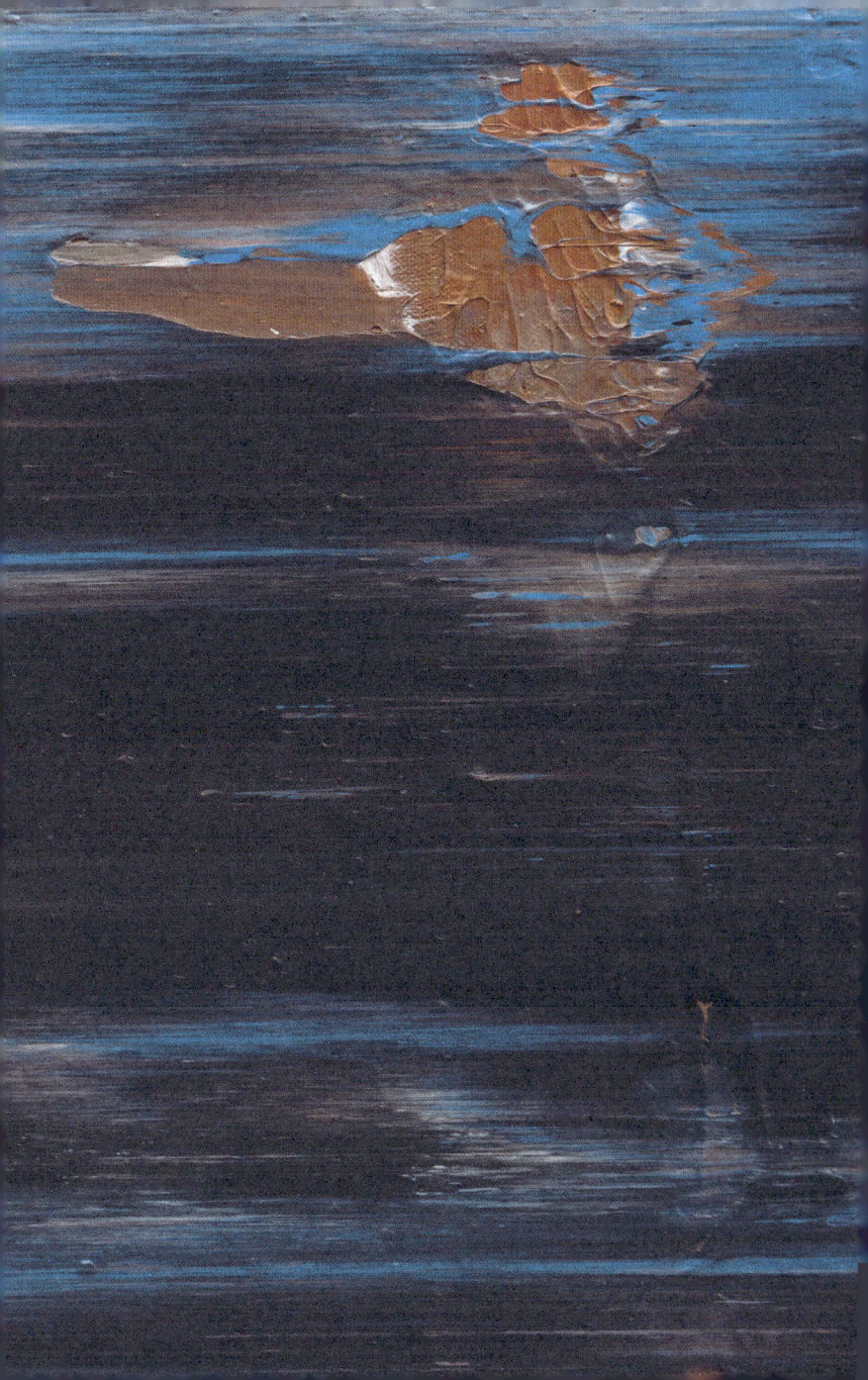

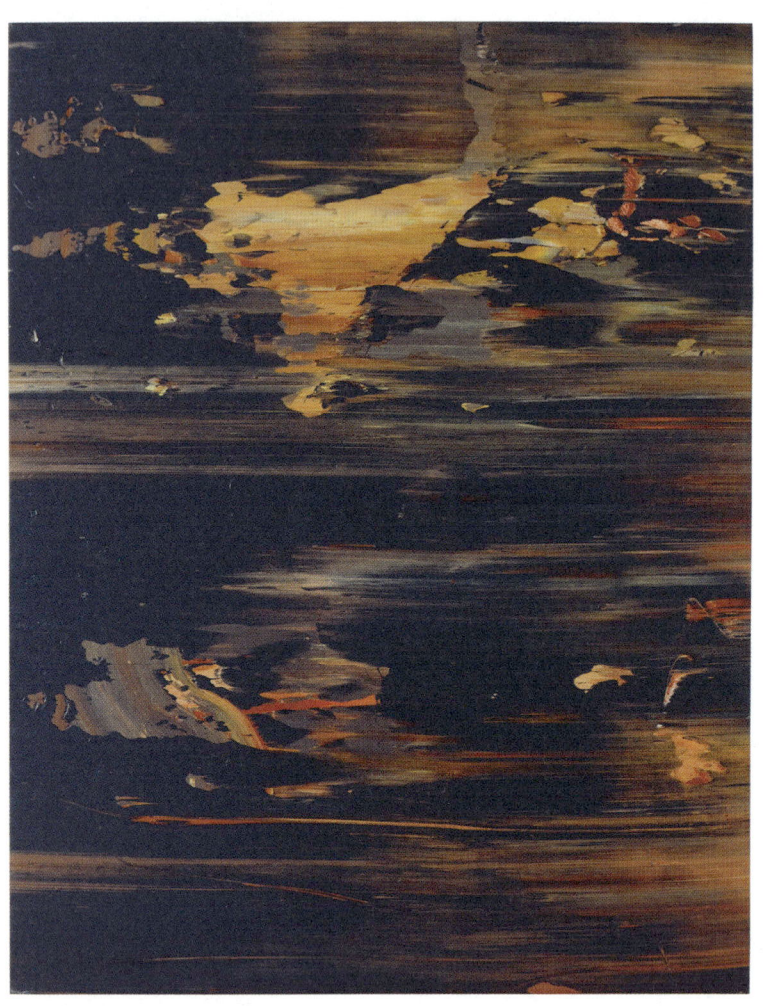

Delacroix's Palette, 1974. Oil on canvas, 72½ × 57⅛ in. (184 × 145 cm)

Materials and Making

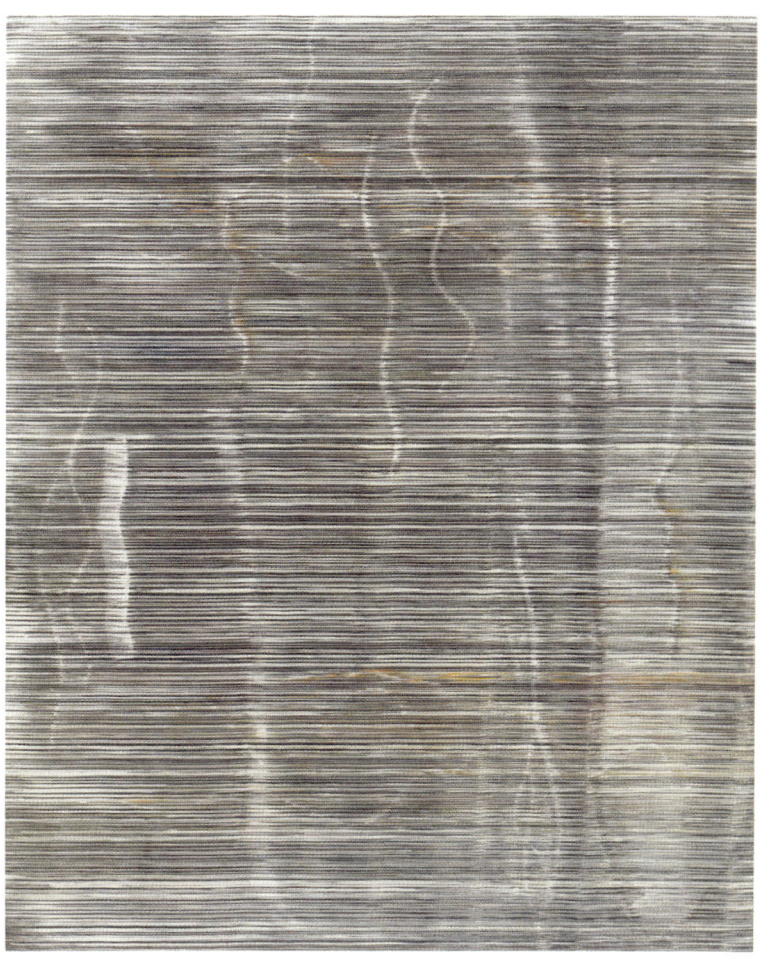

The Speedchaser, 1975. Acrylic on canvas, 72 × 60 in. (182.9 × 152.4 cm)

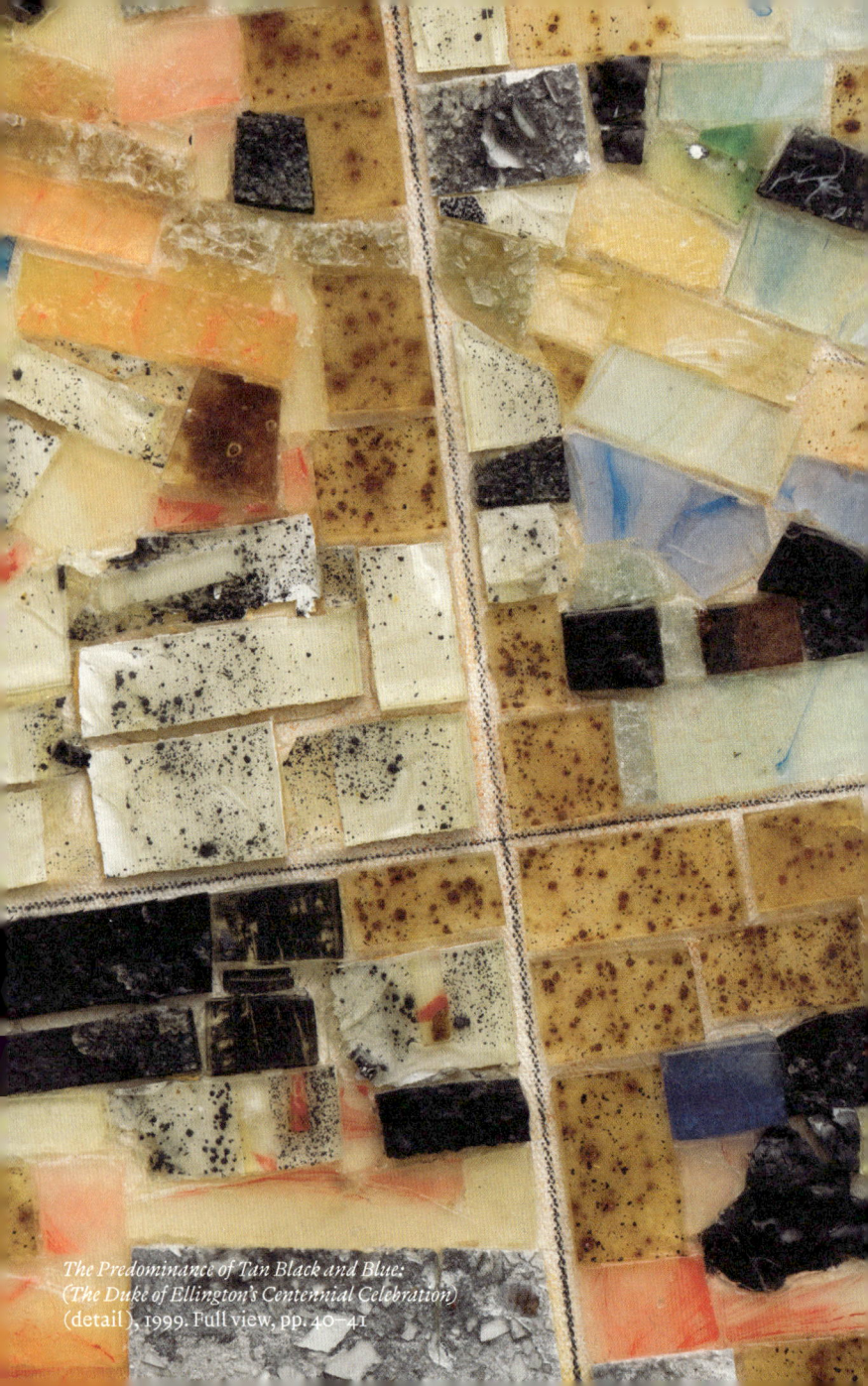

The Predominance of Tan Black and Blue:
(The Duke of Ellington's Centennial Celebration)
(detail), 1999. Full view, pp. 40–41

"A Tool for Structuring Molecular Perception"

The paintings Whitten made with his developers were the first real fruits of his exploration of the materiality of paint; an even more radical invention was to come in the 1990s, which took him away entirely from using brush-like implements to working like a bricklayer instead.

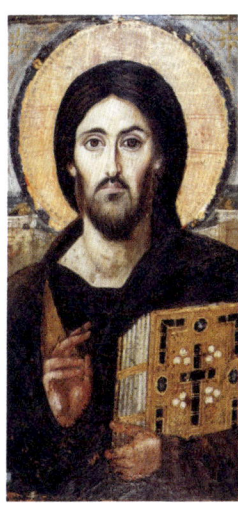

Christ Pantocrator, Saint Catherine's Monastery, Sinai, Egypt, sixth century

In many of Whitten's works from this later period, the image is made up of small bits of blocks. Whitten came to call these blocks tesserae, named after the small stone tiles used in the ancient world to make mosaics. He had long been interested in the materiality of paint itself, and after studying mosaics throughout the Mediterranean world, including Italy and Egypt, he became captivated by the way each tile traps and focuses light differently. Of his visit to Saint Catherine's, the oldest monastery on Mount Sinai, Whitten said, "About midway through the service that mosaic starts coming alive. It was built to put you in the presence of God."

Whitten merged this visceral experience of the art of the ancient world with the work of scientists like Benoit Mandelbrot on fractal geometry and began to focus the reflection of light in his own paintings, too. In a studio note from 2012, he wrote, "My use of acrylic tesserae is a unit. The tesserae provided me with a tool for structuring molecular perception."

Whitten made his tesserae by laying down large swaths of acrylic paint that he then cut into small pieces. He used acrylic slip to carefully adhere these tiles onto the canvas at specific angles to control how each would catch or reflect light and, in turn, how the painting as a whole would do so. It was with this technique that he made many of his iconic paintings, particularly those dedicated to historical figures such as musicians Duke Ellington, Ella Fitzgerald, Milton "Bags" Jackson, and Prince; artists Louise Bourgeois and Arshile Gorky; and athletes like Joe DiMaggio.

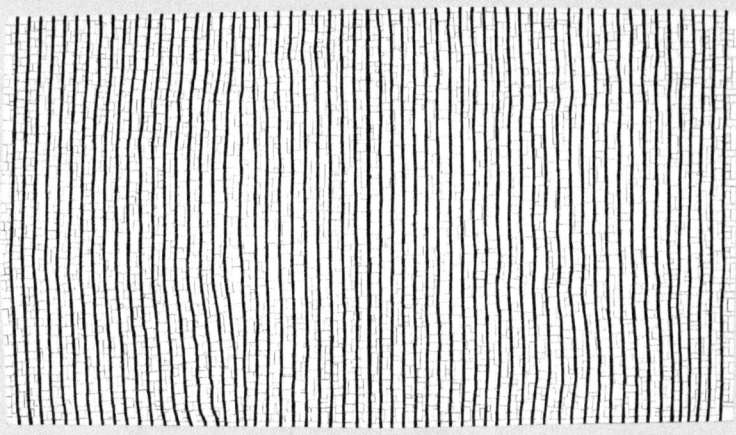

Yankee Clipper: For Joe DiMaggio, 1999
Acrylic on canvas, 52½ × 96 in. (133.4 × 243.8 cm)

In Whitten's *Yankee Clipper: For Joe DiMaggio* (1999) a broken milk-white background is serrated by fractured black stripes. The cracks on both layers offer a system as firmly regimented (the lines) as it is softly corporeal (their buckling). This painting is a triumph of Whitten's choice of material, which permits such paradoxes and effaces the hand that created it. *Yankee Clipper* was inspired by a newspaper photo of a New York Yankee playing baseball; reflecting on the work, Whitten wrote: "The painting is somatic, i.e., it references the body. I discovered asymmetrical black and white stripe patterns in the Yankees' pinstriped uniforms, formed by the twisting and bending of the body under extreme physical exertion. These black and white, asymmetrical, pinstriped patterns gave me a beautiful opening to bypass the historical reference of modernist stripe paintings. The painting is whimsical."

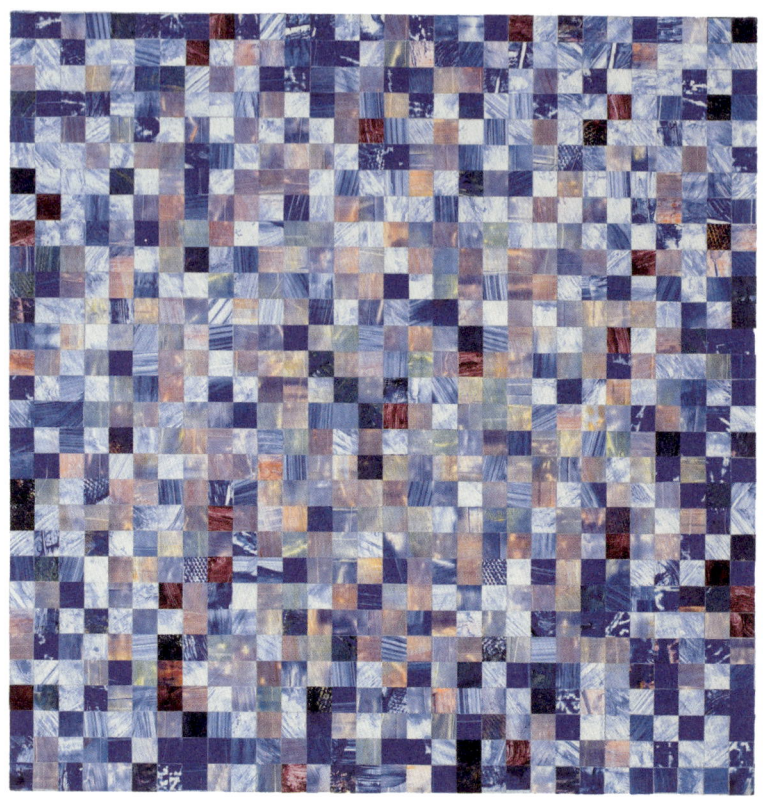

Confirmation, 1990. Acrylic on canvas, 30⅛ × 30⅛ in. (76.5 × 76.5 cm)

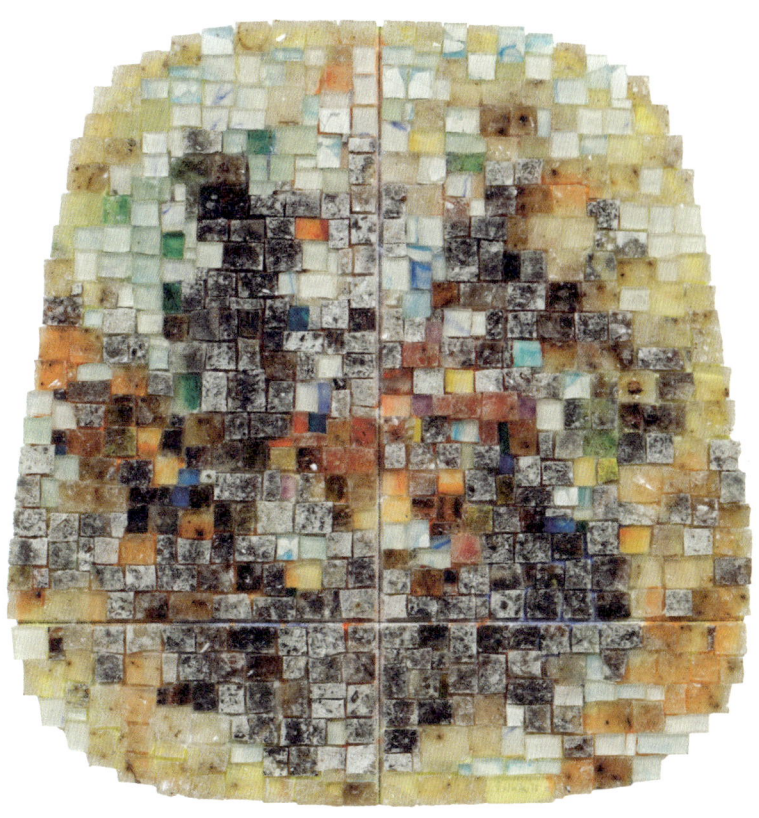

Ella II: For Ella Fitzgerald, 1997. Acrylic and recycled glass on wood, 16 × 15 in. (40.6 × 38.1 cm)

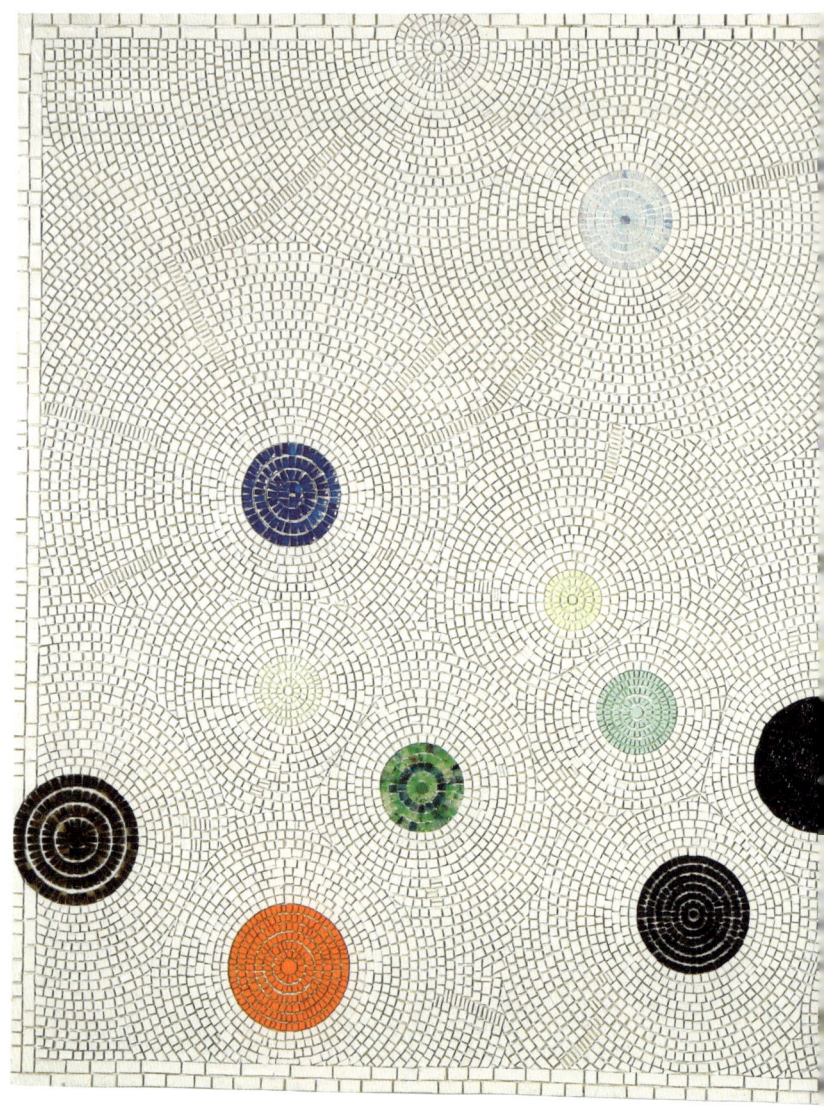

Vibrations For Milt "Bags" Jackson, 1999. Acrylic on canvas, 59½ × 96¼ in.
(151.1 × 244.5 cm)

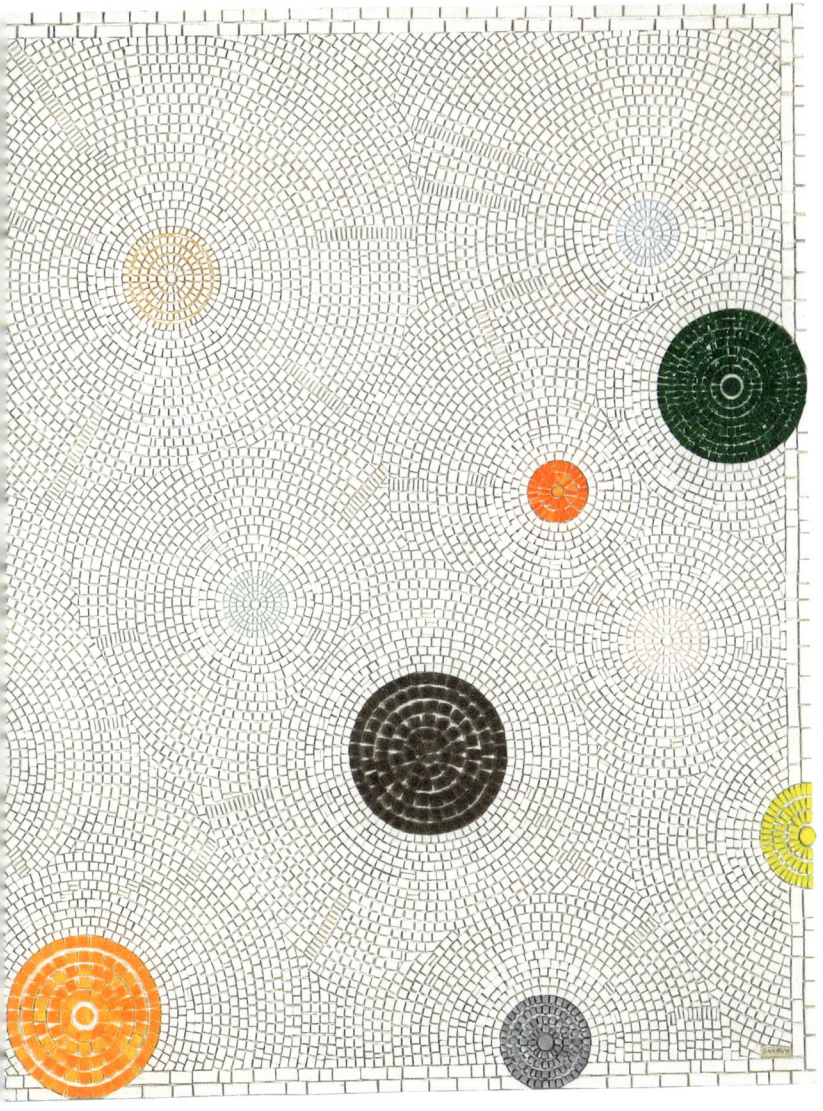

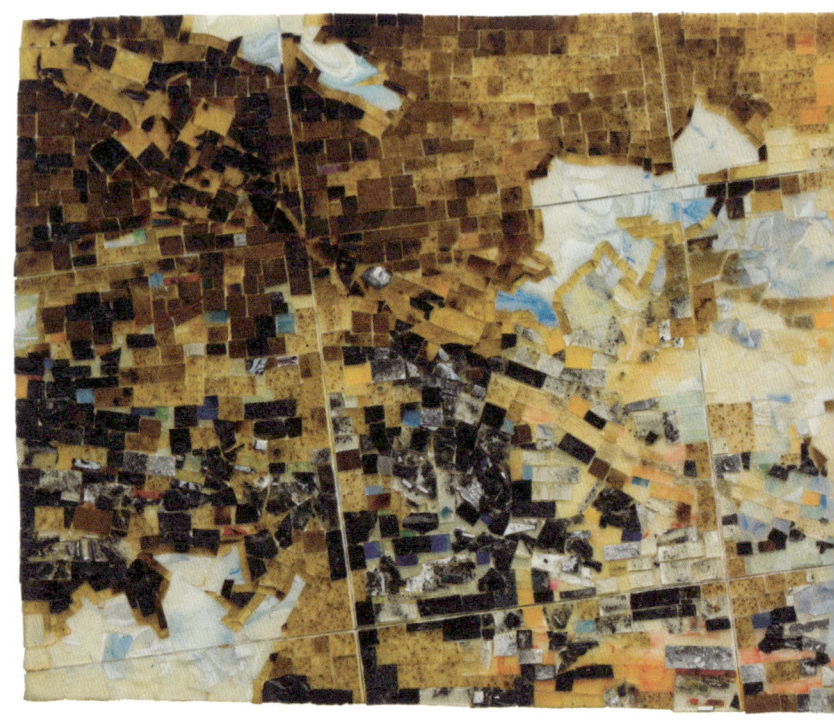

The Predominance of Tan Black and Blue: (The Duke of Ellington's Centennial Celebration), 1999. Acrylic on canvas, 31½ × 81¼ in. (80 × 206.4 cm). Detail, p. 32

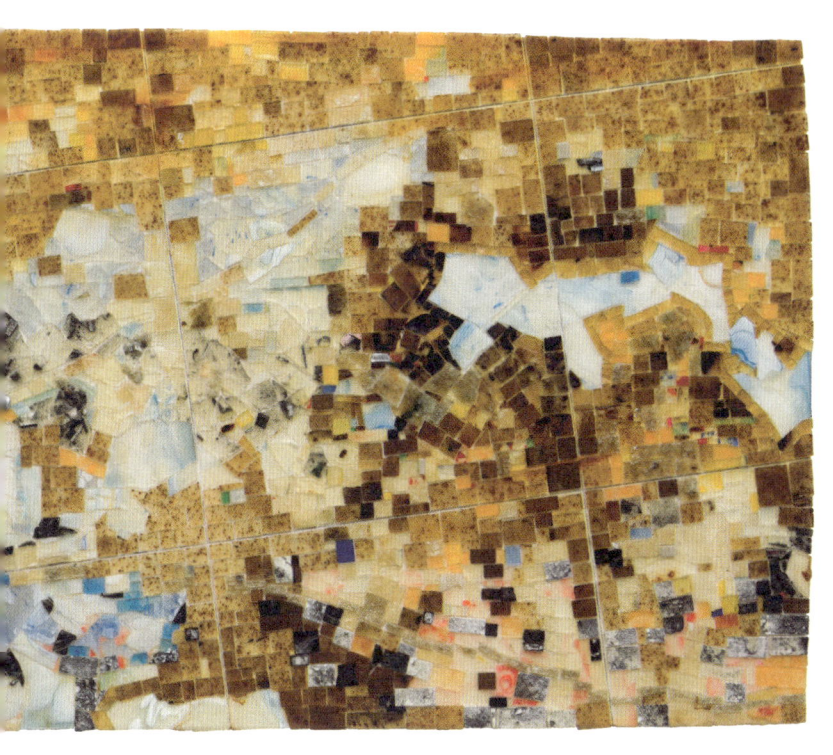

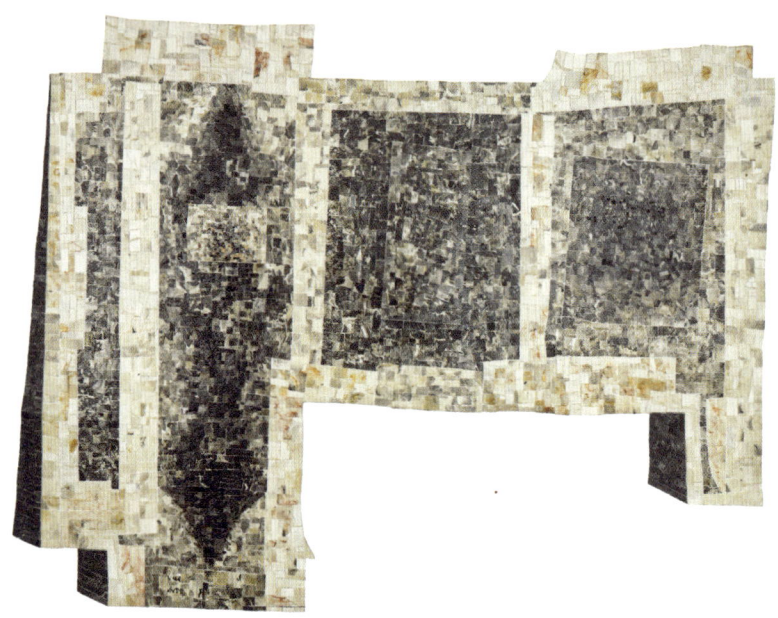

Windows Of The Mind: A Monument Dedicated To The Power Of Painting, 1995.
Acrylic on canvas, 102 × 136 in. (259.1 × 345.4 cm). Detail opposite

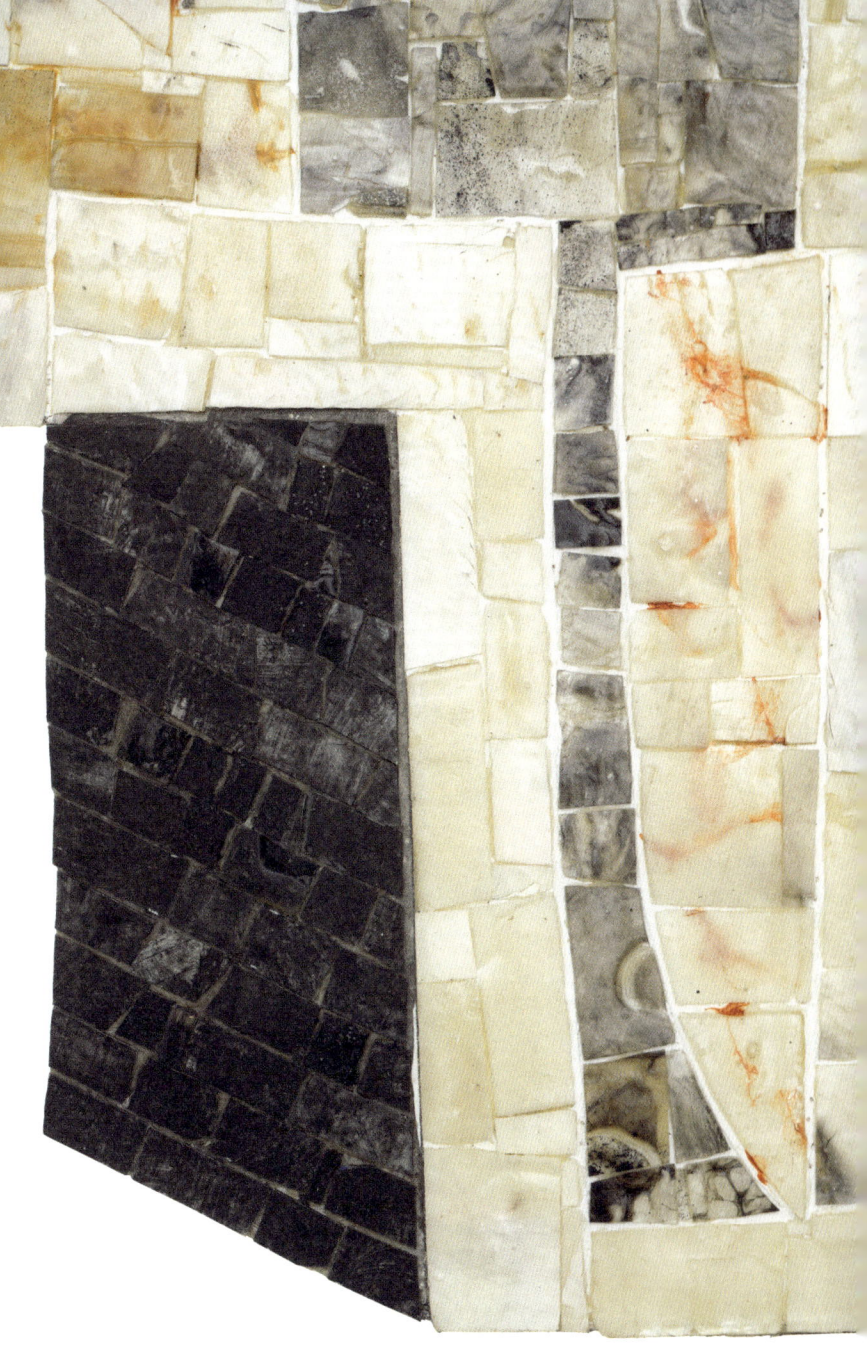

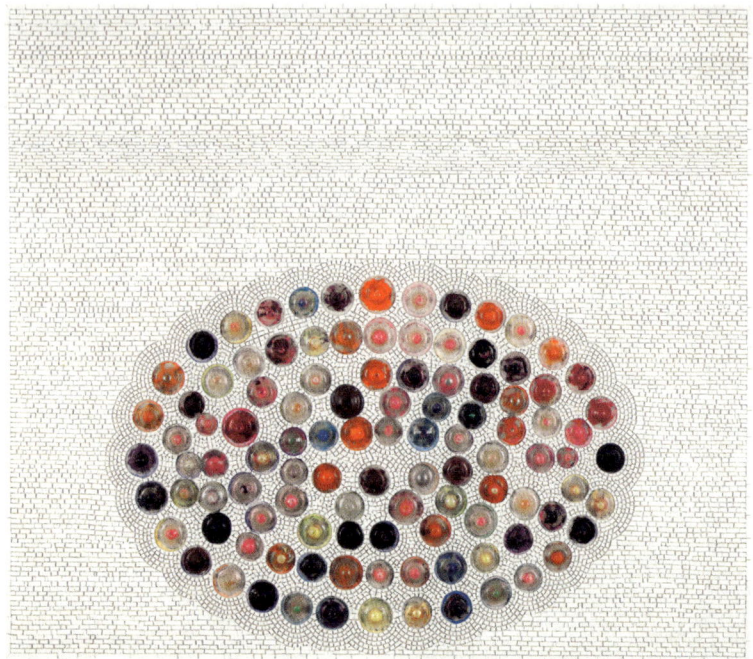

Saint Louise AKA The Tittie Painting for Louise Bourgeois, 2010. Acrylic collage on canvas, 64¼ × 76 in. (163.3 × 193 cm). Detail opposite

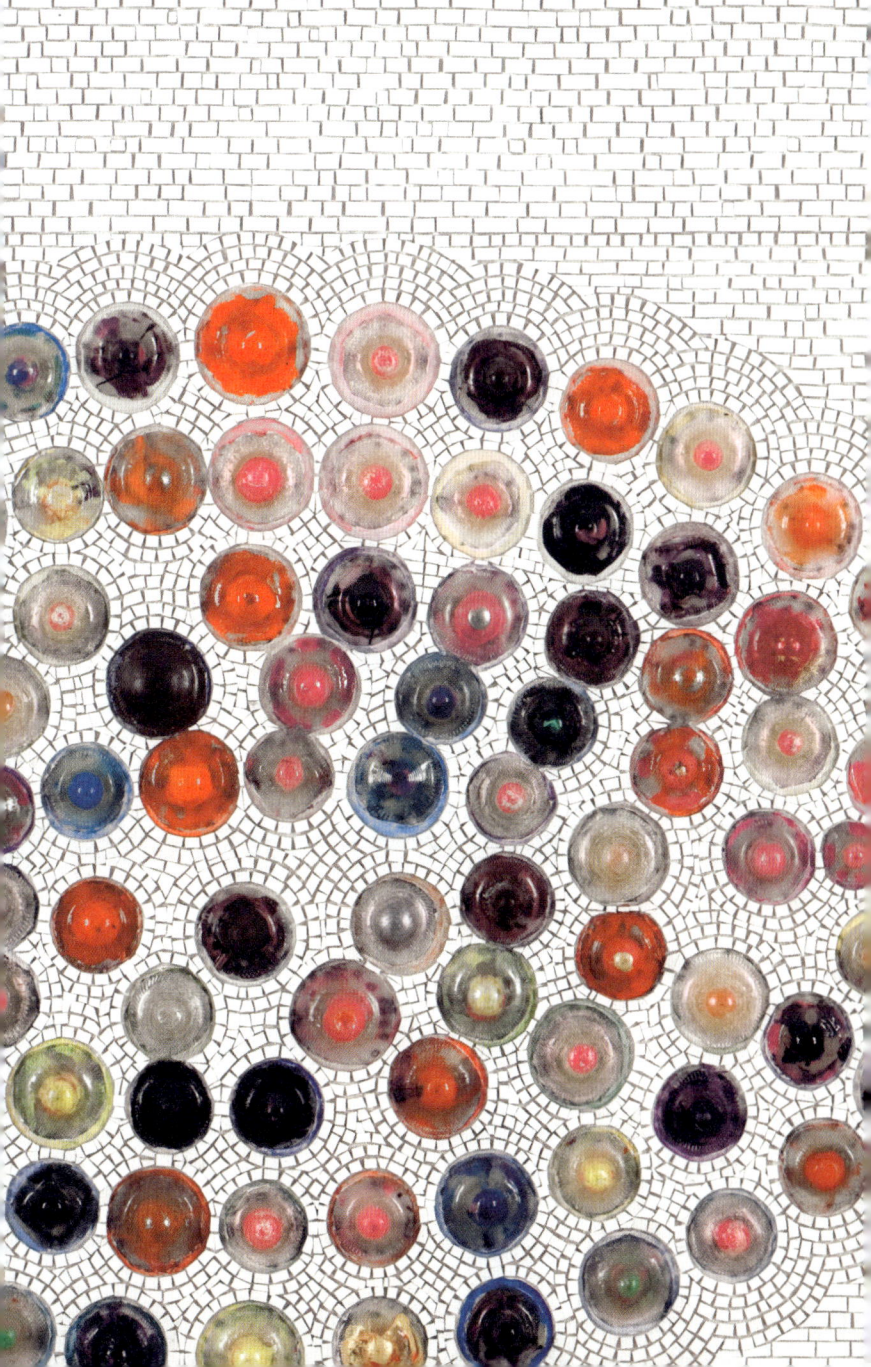

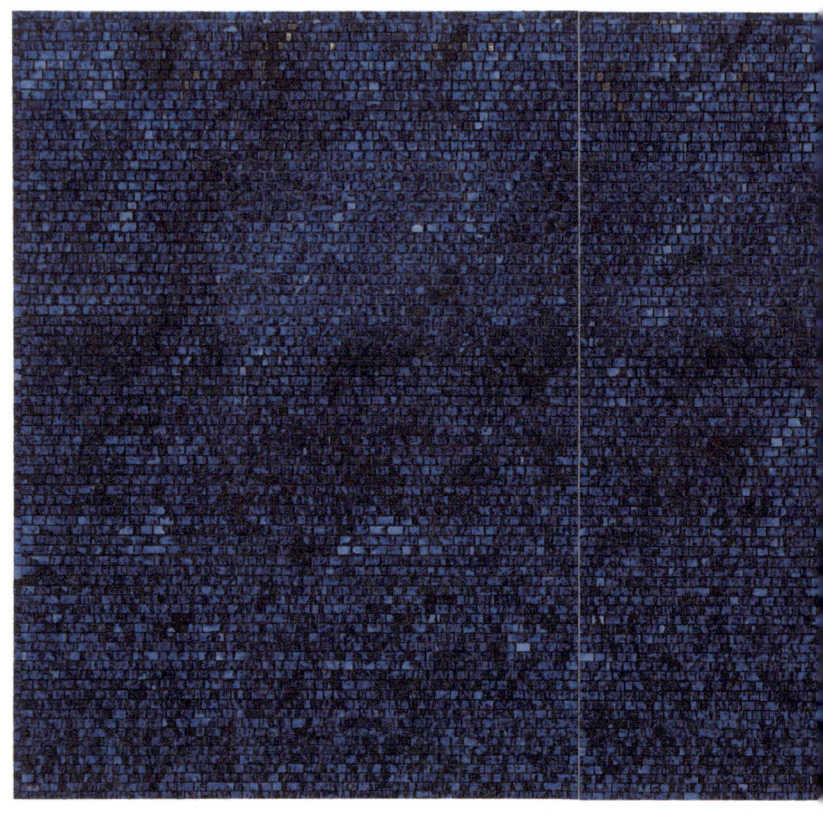

Quantum Wall (*A Gift for Prince*), 2016. Acrylic on canvas with Tivar, 84 × 190 in. (213.4 × 482.6 cm). Detail, pp. 48–49

Materials and Making

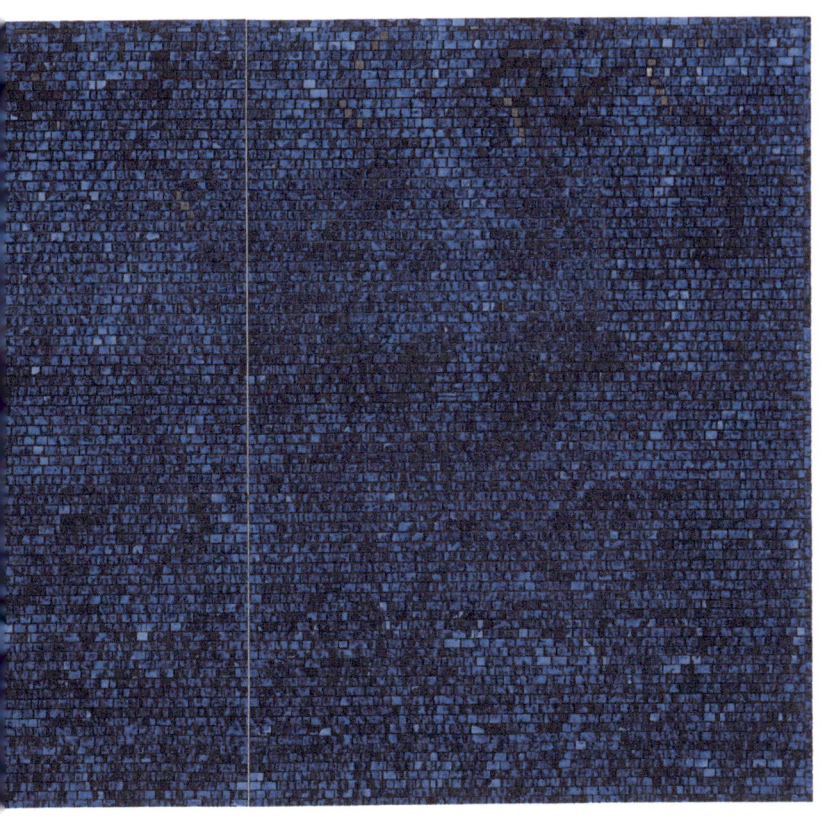

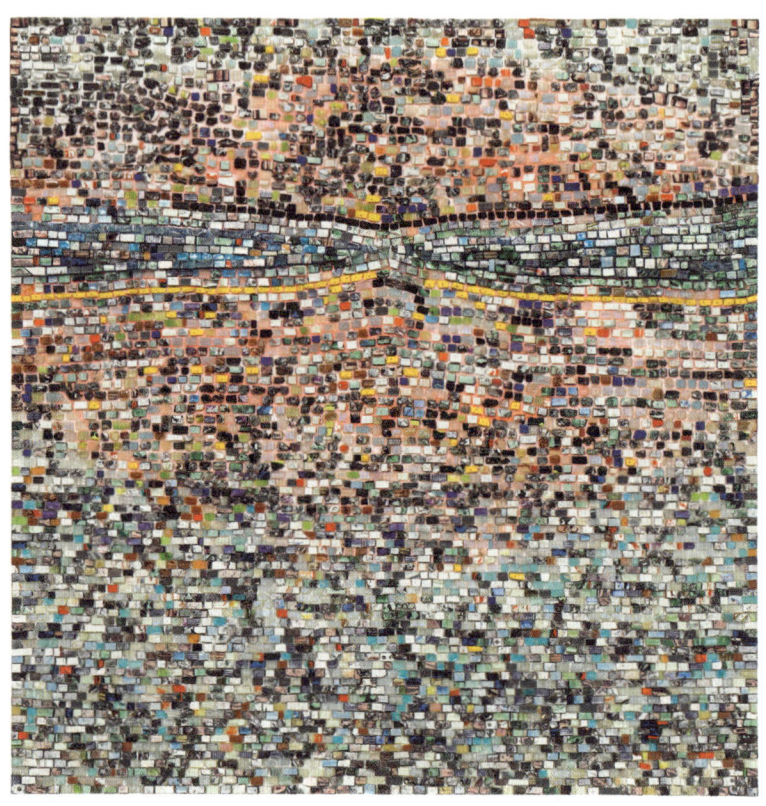

Quantum Wall, VIII (For Arshile Gorky, My First Love in Painting), 2017. Acrylic on canvas, 48¼ × 48¼ in. (122.6 × 122.6 cm). Detail opposite

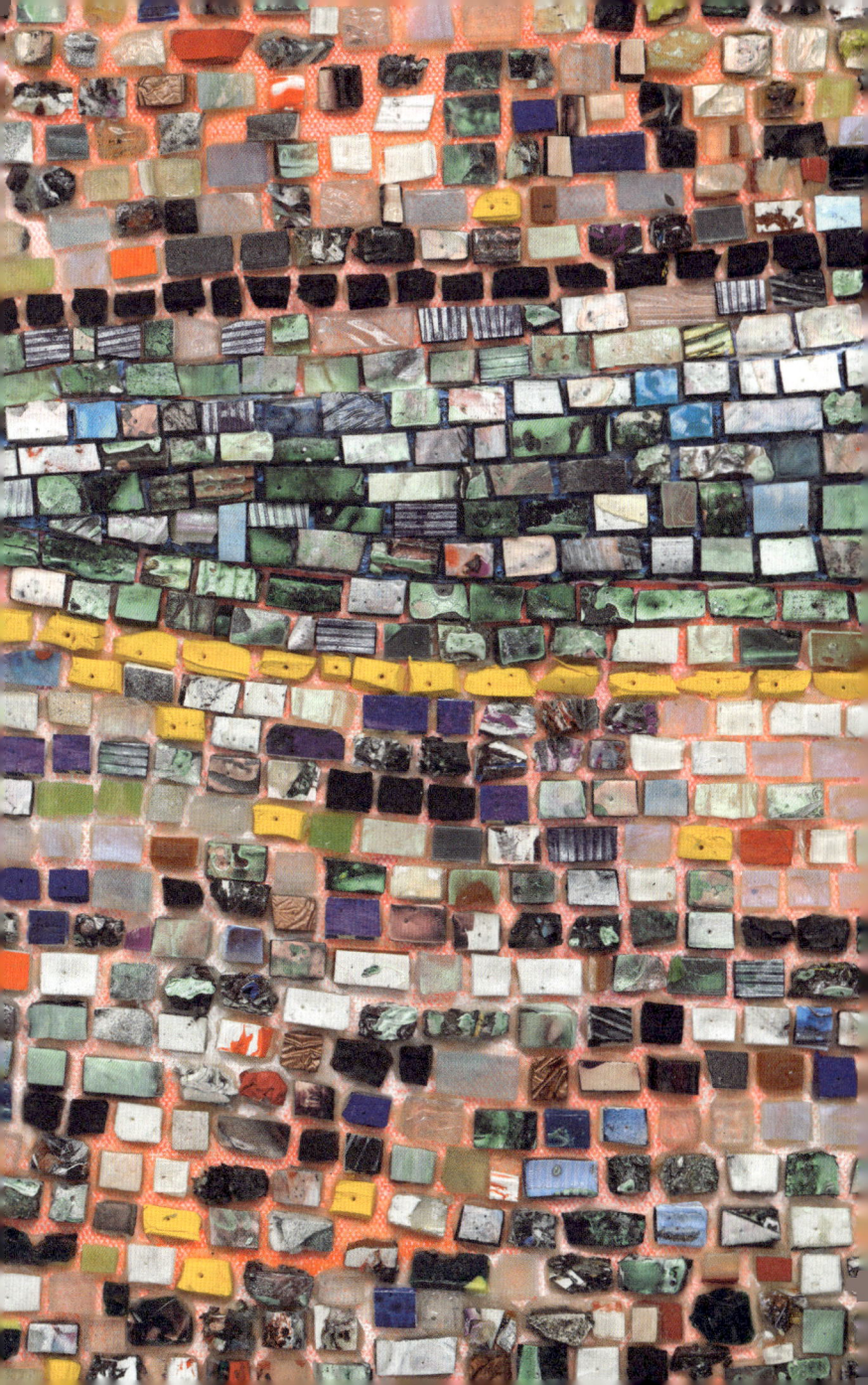

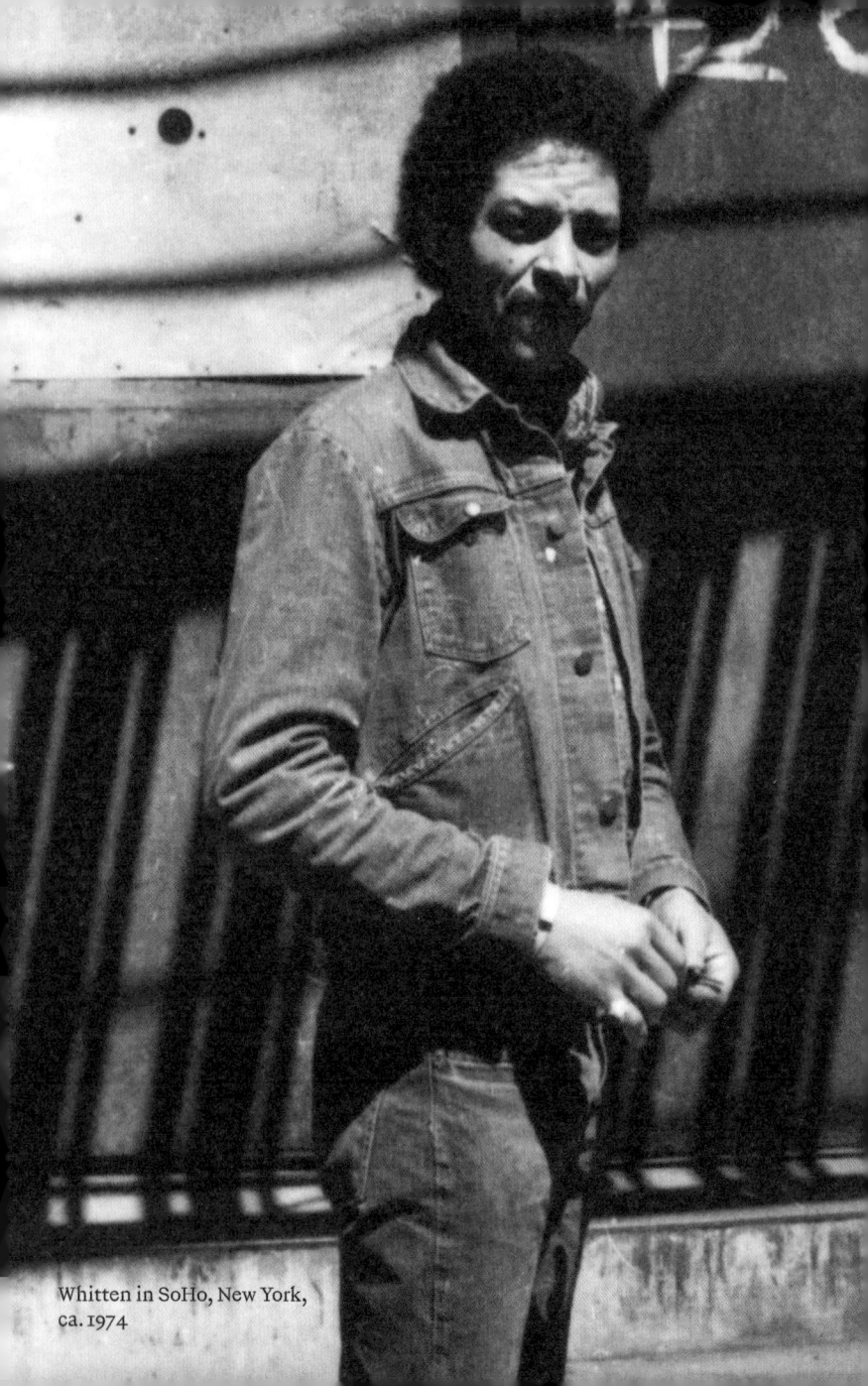

Whitten in SoHo, New York,
ca. 1974

Beginnings

Whitten was born on December 5, 1939, to a seamstress and a coalminer in Bessemer, Alabama. His mother, Annie B. Whitten, had four children from a previous marriage when she married his father, Mose, with whom she had three more children, including Jack. Coming of age in the South during the Jim Crow era, when intense racial discrimination was literally the law of the land, Whitten was educated in a segregated school system. He first displayed artistic interests in high school, playing the tenor saxophone and designing the posters for school dances.

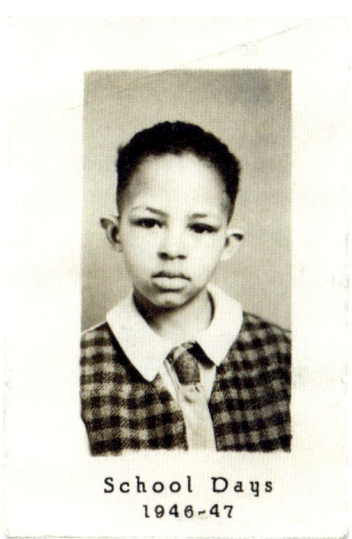

Whitten as a student at Carver Elementary School, Bessemer, Alabama, 1946–47

In 1957, at eighteen, he enrolled in the United States Air Force Reserve Officer Training Corps at the historic Tuskegee Institute (now Tuskegee University), where he majored in premedical studies. A work-study job as a janitor helped pay his tuition, and his duties included cleaning the laboratory of the Black agronomist George Washington Carver. Whitten remembered this period fondly: "I actually handled his stuff. This deeply affected me." That same year, Whitten encountered another influential force in his life: when traveling to nearby Montgomery to play in Tuskegee's marching band at a football game against Alabama State, he heard Dr. Martin Luther King Jr. speak during the historic boycott of the city's segregated buses.

Whitten, however, began to grow disillusioned with the path he was on at Tuskegee. In 1959, he "had a revelation during an early morning ROTC class, where I stood out of my seat and said 'What am I doing here?'" One of his professors suggested Whitten instead pursue his interest in art at Southern University in Baton Rouge, Louisiana, or Cooper Union in New York. Whitten transferred to the former, and, inspired by Dr. King's speech and the burgeoning civil rights movement, became one of the organizers of a civil rights march in Baton Rouge. The march unfortunately turned violent, and Whitten fled the South for his safety. He set his sights on New York (he had first traveled there in the summers of 1958 and 1959 to earn money to pay his tuition), and he arrived in 1960, just in time for that year's Cooper Union entrance exam.

It was at Cooper Union that Whitten really began to flourish. He studied with some of the greatest artists of the time and, outside of school, met and was mentored by Norman Lewis, Jacob Lawrence, and Romare Bearden. He also spent time at the Cedar Bar with Beat writers like Jack Kerouac and Allen Ginsberg as well as Abstract Expressionists like de Kooning, Franz Kline, Newman, and Mark Rothko. He witnessed many historic jazz performances, sitting at Kenny Dorham's feet at the Five Spot Cafe, where he watched Ornette Coleman

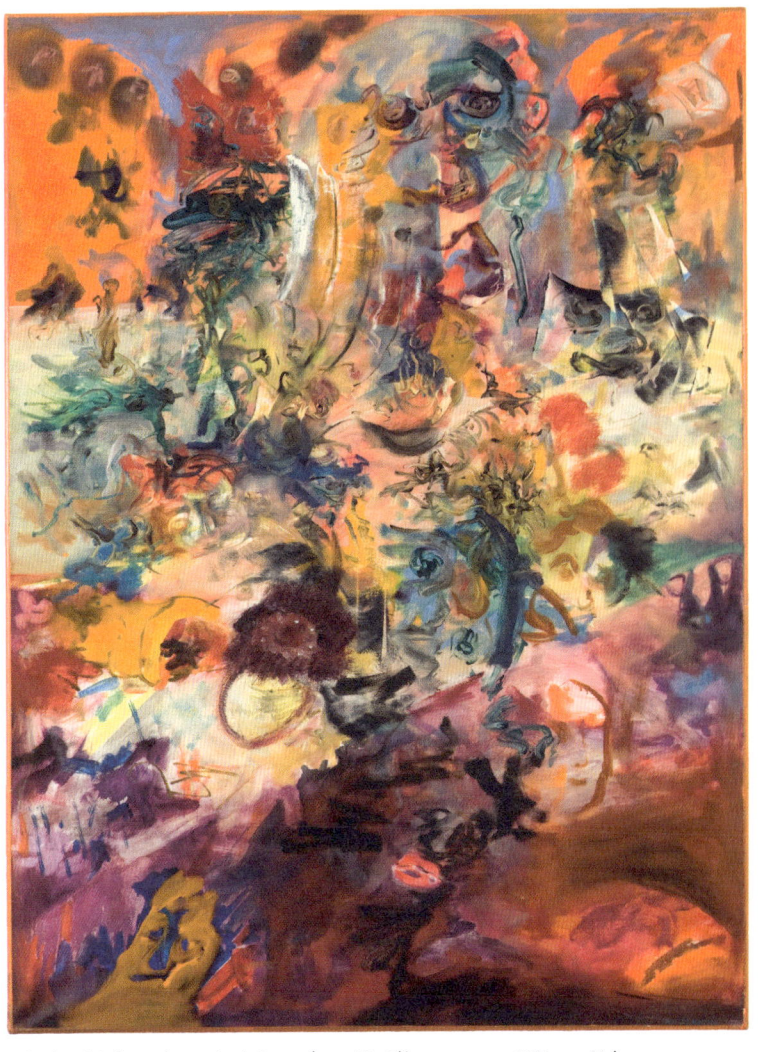

King's Wish (Martin Luther's Dream), 1968. Oil on canvas, 68⅛ × 51⅜ in. (173 × 130.5 cm)

get chased off the stand, and meeting John Coltrane during a visit to the Blue Coronet with his brother Tommy, also a jazz musician. It was in this world that Whitten started to come into his own, defining himself as an artist. And it was also here that he began to find his community.

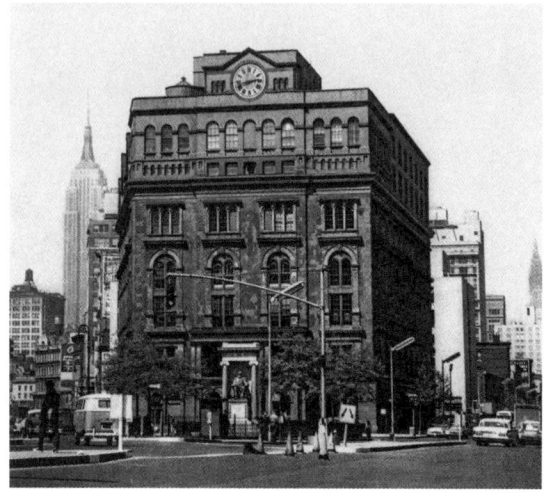

Cooper Union, New York, ca. 1962

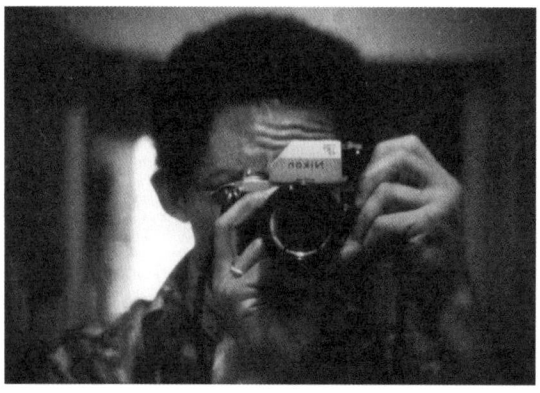

Whitten, ca. 1960s

Life and Work

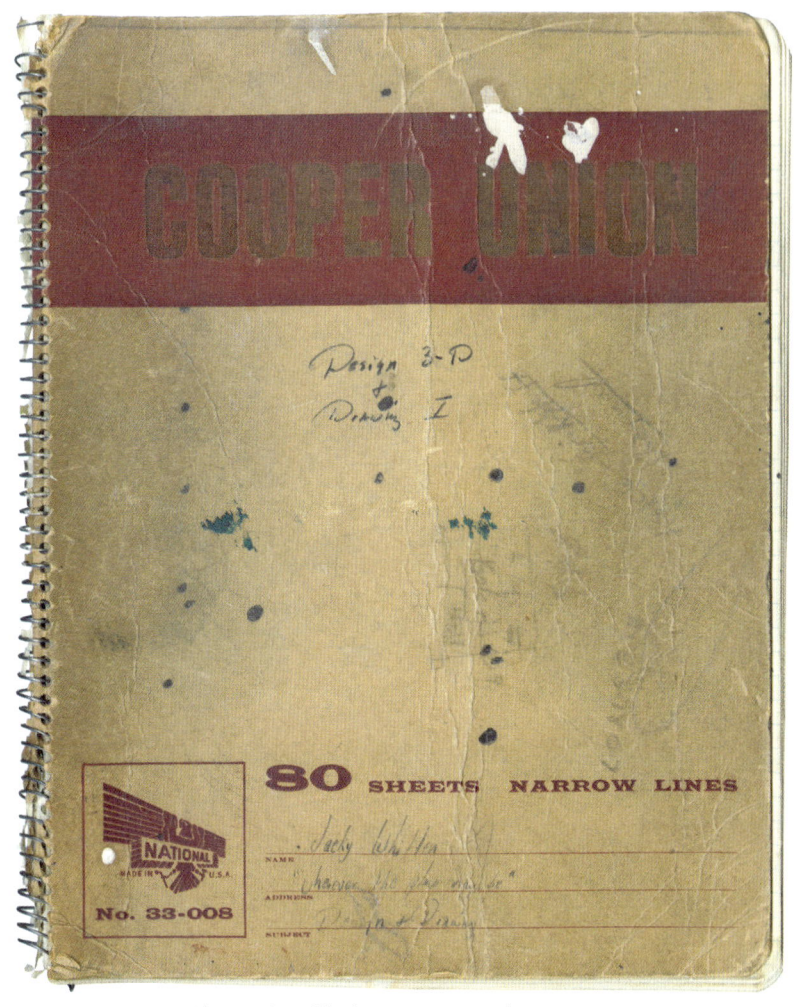

A notebook of Whitten's from his time at Cooper Union, ca. 1962

Contemporaries

As Whitten was inventing his way out of the established modes of painting he had practiced in his younger years, other artists were also trying to reimagine prevailing aesthetics. Whether discussing art or simply getting together as friends, it was among these peers—many of whom would become key figures in American art—that Whitten built his community.

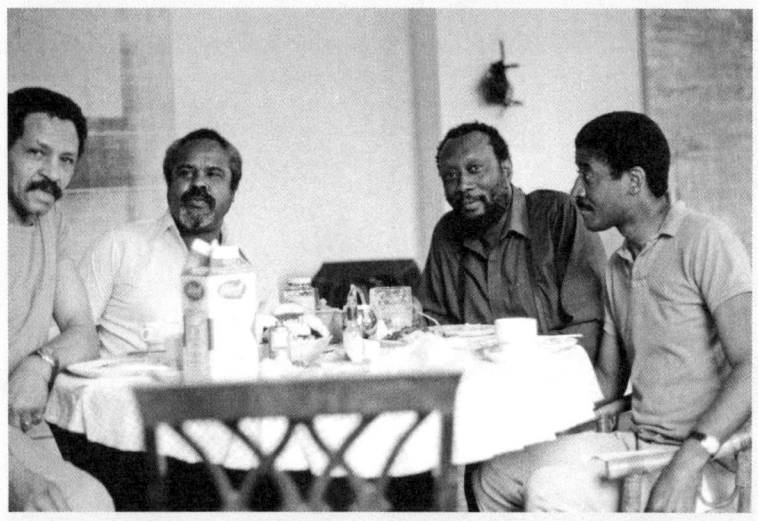

From left: Jack Whitten, Mel Edwards, Frank Bowling, and Bill Williams in the living room of the Whitten family home on Lispenard Street, New York, 1983. One of Edwards's Lynch Fragments can be seen on the wall behind them.

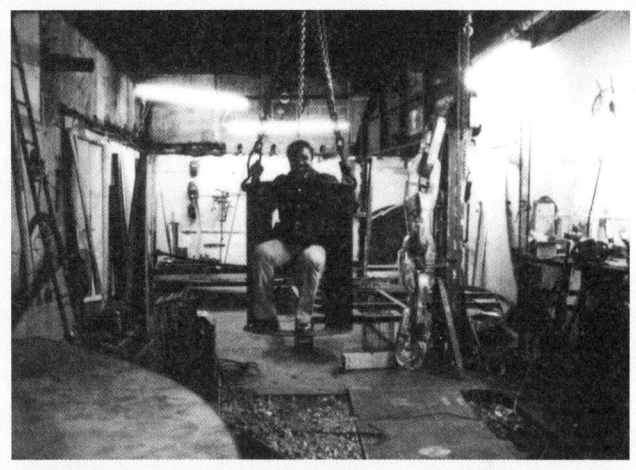
Whitten's photograph of Melvin Edwards in his studio, ca. 1980s

Melvin Edwards

Whitten and Edwards first met in 1968, a year after the latter had moved to New York from Los Angeles. Both men's work was exhibited that year in *New Voices: 15 New York Artists*, organized by Ruder & Finn Fine Arts and the Studio Museum in Harlem at American Greetings Gallery in Midtown Manhattan. The two became close friends, bonding over their shared origins in the American South (Edwards was from Texas but had family connections to Alabama, Whitten's home state) and the satisfaction they derived from having a place to escape to outside the United States (Greece for Whitten; Senegal for Edwards). Whenever one man returned from a trip to his second home, he brought back a gift for the other: Edwards once gave Whitten an African adze and Whitten would bring Edwards bottles of the homemade Cretan spirit *raki*. When Whitten married his wife Mary, Edwards was his best man.

Edwards originally trained as a painter but worked as a sculptor. Now considered a pioneer in contemporary American art, he used welded steel, barbed wire, chain, and machine parts to create distinctive three-dimensional installations. Like Whitten, Edwards was formulating a language that responded to the principles and history of abstraction while redefining what was possible in modern sculpture. Indeed, in a 2018 conversation with art historian and curator Katy Siegel at the Baltimore Museum of Art, Edwards reflected that, "if there was ever a lesson for me, and I would say Jack shared this, [it was that] you were free to invent your own game, your own rules, your own methods, and see what it looked like."

Unlike Whitten, however, Edwards's work was more pointedly political: his most famous series, Lynch Fragments (1963–), responded to racial violence in the United States. Drawing inspiration from modernists like Spanish sculptor Julio González and American sculptor David Smith, Edwards's *Some Bright Morning* (1963) sets the tone for the series as a whole: in a mass of welded steel with a patina of rust, a sharp protrusion juts from a circular core like a bird's beak, over which a heavy chain dangles. Installed at Edwards's eye level, the Lynch Fragments demand viewers reckon with the brutality of Black American experience.

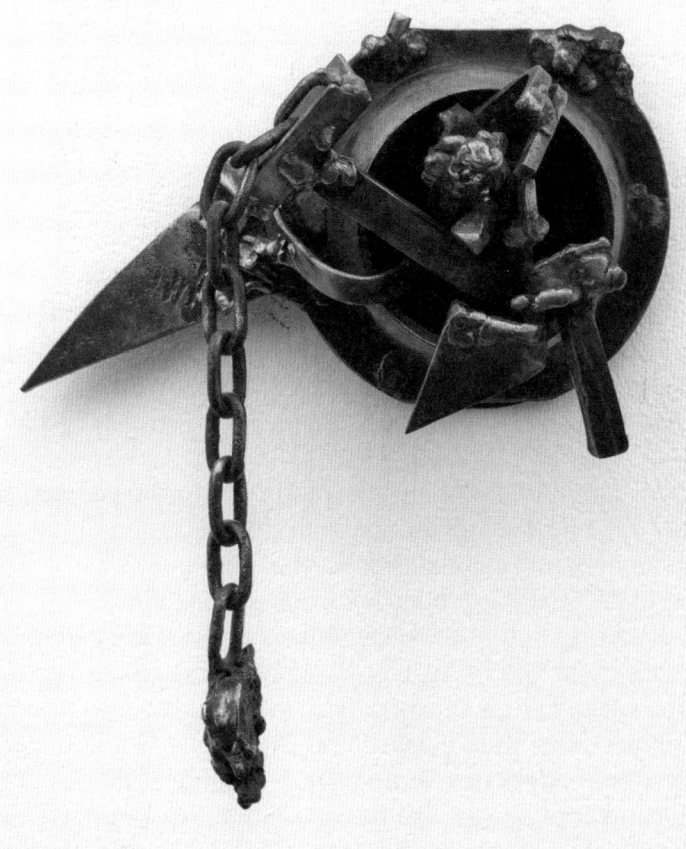

Melvin Edwards, *Some Bright Morning*, 1963. Welded steel, 14¼ × 9¼ × 5 in.
(36.2 × 23.5 × 12.7 cm)

William T. Williams

Whitten was not the only artist in his milieu reworking
the possibilities of painting. In 1968, he met William
T. Williams, and, with Edwards and the British-Guyanese
artist Frank Bowling, the four enjoyed a comradeship,
even while each man's work took a distinct path.

Williams was born into a culture of makers in rural North
Carolina: his family sewed patchwork quilts similar to the
now famous quilts of Gee's Bend, Alabama. The Williamses
moved north to New York when he was four, and with their
support, he enrolled in art school at fourteen. Reflecting
on the origins of his style, Williams reported, "I wasn't
really interested in Abstract Expressionism, and I wasn't
really interested in figuration. I was interested in where
they started, but that's not quite what I wanted. I wanted
to make something that resonated more with heritable
information—'autobiographical information' might
be a better way of saying it."

Williams began to carry his own history onto the canvas,
pioneering a hard-edge abstraction that referenced
the geometry and radical simplicity of his family's
quilts. In *1940* (1970), sharp lines and shapes abut
each other as though they are different materials joined
at their edges. The texture of the canvas resembles
a patchworked piece of cloth, thus avoiding the flat
look of more traditional paintings. The colors—shades
of brown, tan, dark green, and a quiet orange—are
homey and comforting, like the quilts that inspired
them. Williams, much like Whitten, rejected the historical
privileging of the artist's hand—a devotion to the brush—
that pervaded Abstract Expressionism.

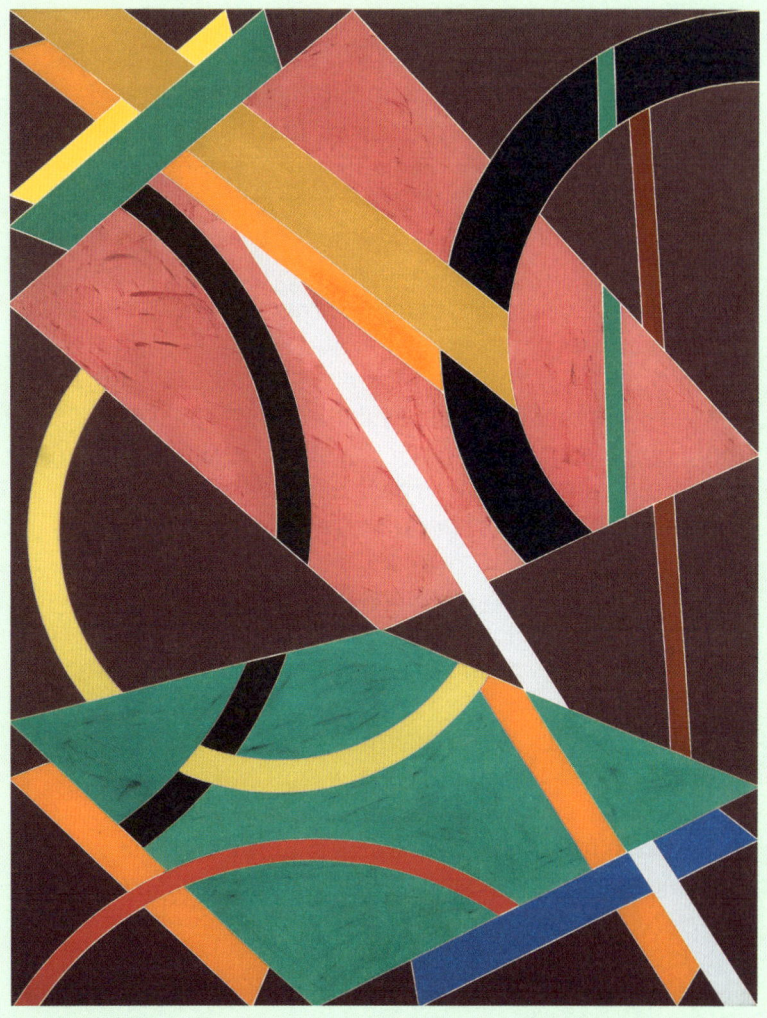

William T. Williams, *1940*, 1970. Acrylic on canvas, 108 × 84 in. (274.3 × 213.4 cm)

Harvey Quaytman

It seems as if every young painter working with abstraction in the 1960s and 1970s knew that the medium was ripe for disruption, though each attacked the problem from a different direction, bringing to it their own eccentricities and way of seeing.

Harvey Quaytman, a friend of Whitten's, employed austere colors and painted his canvases sparely, often starting by mapping out crosses to create topography within an otherwise abstract field. In *Half and Half* (1997), the blacks on the right side of the cross embrace it like a shadow, giving it a certain gravitas, while the whites make the shape feel feathery. It is as if the shape is sinking into and rising from the canvas at the same time. Quaytman innovated ways of working with blends of materials such as acrylic, glass, and rust, to create a range of textures that give his paintings a loamy feel, and he was instrumental in introducing his peers—including Whitten— to the unique color pigments supplied by Georg Kremer.

In 2008, six years after Quaytman's death, Whitten made *E Stamp VI Vouvray (For Harvey Quaytman)*, a painting with nickel yellow and aluminum tesserae arranged in four squares to form a subtle cross in the middle—a reference to Quaytman's favored pictorial device and preference for Vouvray wine. According to notes Whitten made upon the painting's completion, it emanated a "weird light," something that "Harvey would understand." Whitten respected Quaytman as an artist, writing in that same note, "I miss Harvey. I sincerely miss speaking to him about painting. He was one of the few people who understood painting."

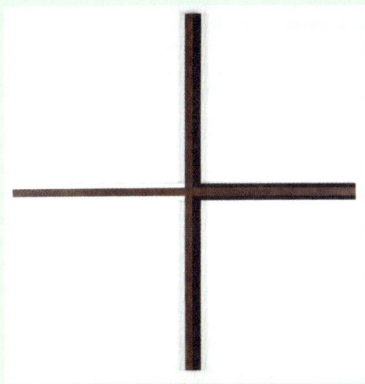

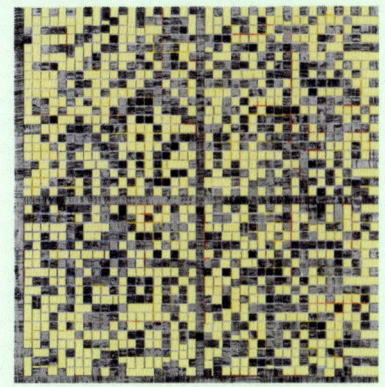

Harvey Quaytman, *Half and Half*, 1997.
Acrylic on canvas, 108½ × 108½ in.
(275.6 × 275.6 cm)

*E Stamp VI Vouvray (For Harvey
Quaytman)*, 2008. Acrylic on canvas,
42 × 42 in. (106.7 × 106.7 cm)

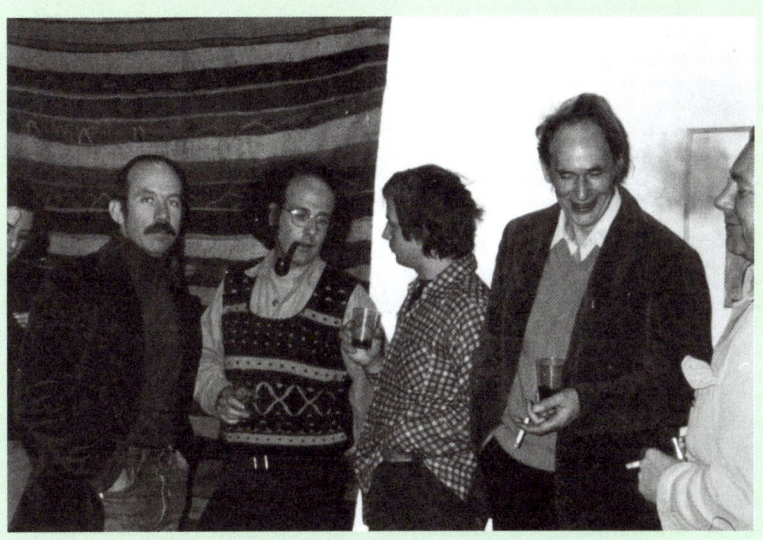

From left: Mary Whitten, Don Lewallen, Harvey Quaytman, Kes Kapkus,
and others at a party in New York, 1974

Norman Lewis

Norman Lewis was known for his calligraphic and atmospheric paintings. A first-generation Abstract Expressionist—and the sole Black artist in that cohort—he worked in the prevailing style from which Whitten wanted to escape. Nonetheless, Lewis was in many ways a source of direction for the younger artist.

In 1962, when the two men met through Romare Bearden, Lewis had a live-work studio in Harlem (where he was deeply involved in the local community) and didn't have commercial gallery representation. Whitten peppered Lewis with all the questions bothering him: What were the effects of racism on his work? What did it mean to be one of the few Black painters working with abstraction in the 1960s? And how could one survive financially as a Black artist? Lewis, who had been largely ignored by collectors despite his numerous awards and prestigious exhibitions, was helpful in many ways but had no solution to the problem of money. Initially mentor and mentee, the men became friends, and Lewis (together with Ouida Bramwell, his fiancée at the time) even visited Whitten in Greece.

Whitten thought the world had something important to glean from Lewis's work, particularly in the new form it gave to Black aesthetics. In 2015, Whitten said of Lewis, "here is a man who is clarifying through abstraction the notion of Black sensibility." Whitten paid homage to Lewis in several paintings, including *Norman Lewis Triptych I*, made in 1985, in which a dark background is enlivened by spots of blues, reds, yellows, and pinks dancing across a grid that resembles a screen, the information just on the verge of cohering into an image.

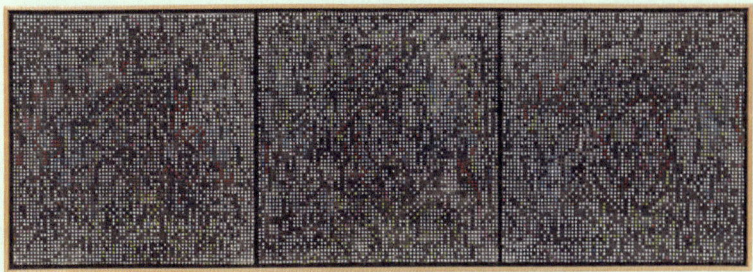

Norman Lewis Triptych I, 1985. Oil and acrylic on canvas, 27 × 80¼ in.
(68.6 × 203.8 cm)

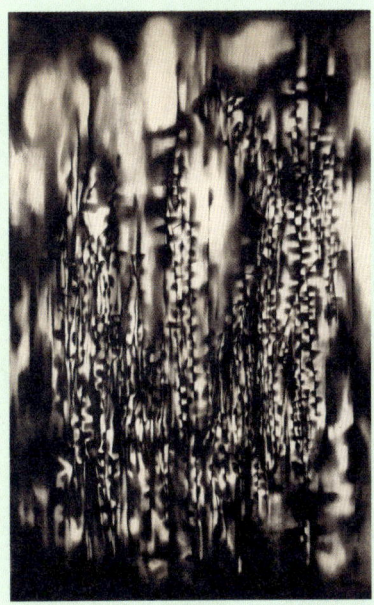

Norman Lewis, *Every Atom Glows:*
Electrons in Luminous Vibration, 1951.
Oil on canvas 54 × 35 in. (137.2 × 88.9 cm)

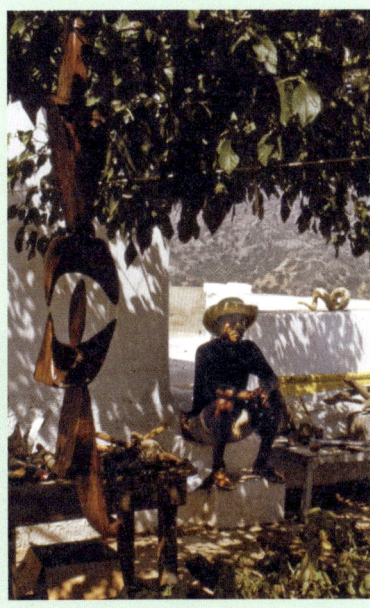

Norman Lewis with a sculpture
by Whitten, Agia Galini, Crete, 1973

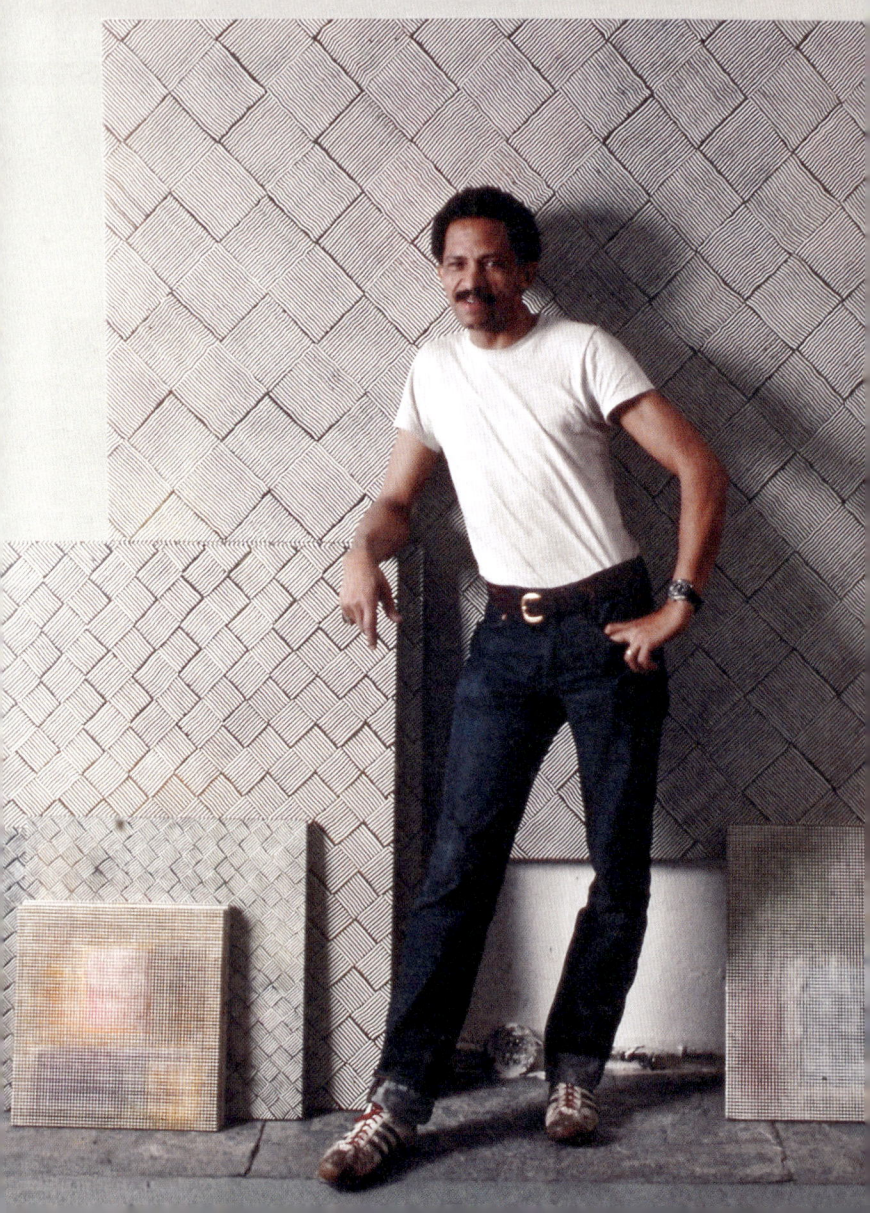

Whitten with the paintings *The Annunciation*, *Ascension*, *DNA*, *Formal Relay*, and *Persian Echo* (all 1979) in his Crosby Street studio, New York, 1979

Studio, Laboratory, Shrine, Home

Whitten's studios doubled not only as workshops but as archives of history and memory, as well. During his time in New York, he had several: first in the East Village at 369 East Tenth Street, where he also lived; then, starting in 1962, at 36 Lispenard Street in TriBeCa, where he lived and worked until he and his wife Mary moved into a loft at 426 Broome Street in SoHo that she had been renting as a studio; in 1972, they began living again on Lispenard Street after a renovation there, and Whitten took over Broome Street as his studio; later in the 1970s, he moved his studio to 40 Crosby Street, also in SoHo; in the 1980s, he began working again from Lispenard Street; and finally, in 2003, he relocated his studio to Queens.

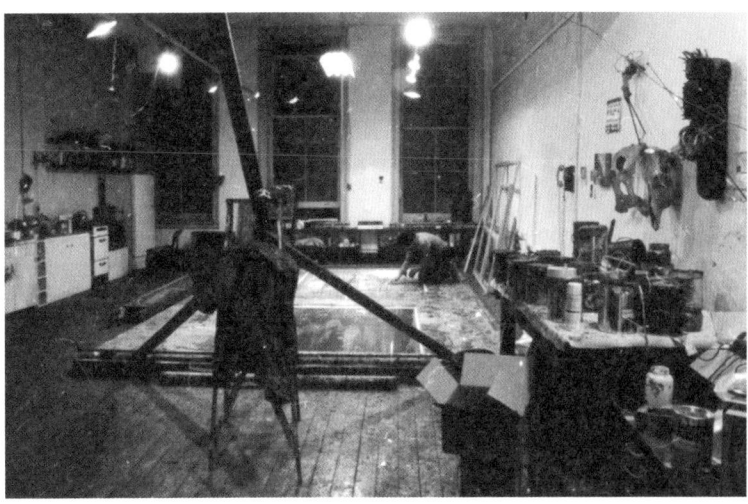

Whitten in his Broome Street studio, New York, early 1970s. *The Black Christ* (1967) is hanging on the wall at right

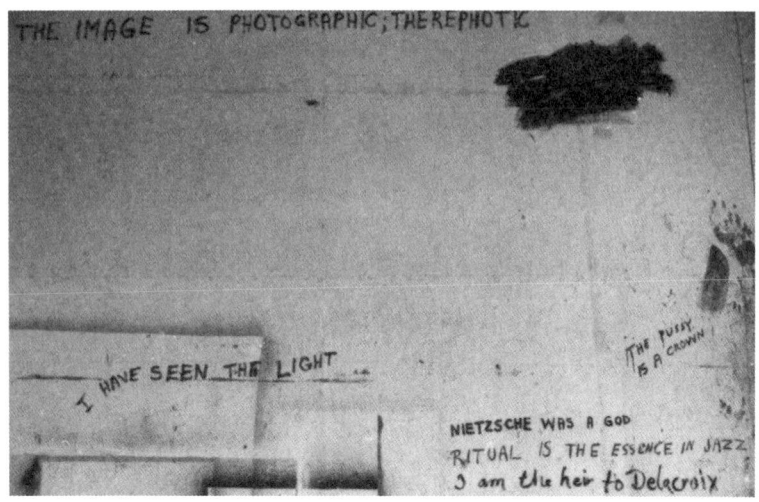

Writing on Whitten's Crosby Street studio wall, ca. 1976–78

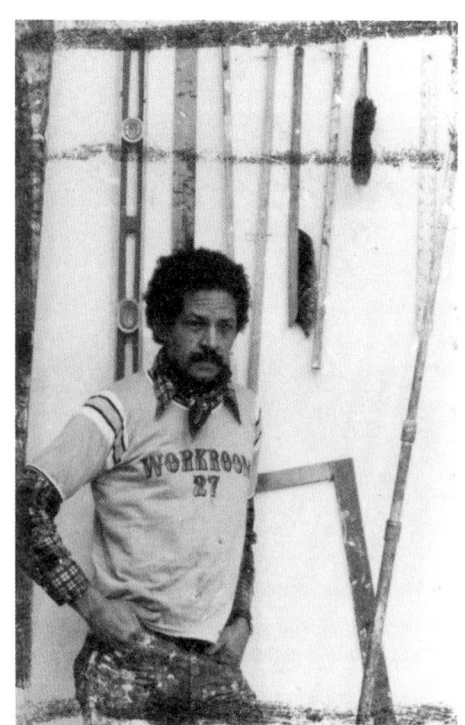

Whitten in his Crosby Street
studio, ca. 1974–75

36 Lispenard Street had a notable history before Whitten moved in: the century prior, that address was home to abolitionist publisher David Ruggles and a "station" on the Underground Railroad, the secret network of safe houses that helped enslaved people of the American South escape to freedom in the north. Ruggles offered shelter to an estimated six hundred people fleeing slavery, including the abolitionist Frederick Douglass, who passed through in 1838. When Whitten arrived in 1962, 36 Lispenard Street—which had since been rebuilt—was an A.I.R. (Artist in Residence) building, a designation that allowed artists to live and work in buildings that had been zoned for industrial use. He initially lived on the second floor, and when he and Mary moved back in 1972, they began renting the third floor, as well.

In 1980, just three weeks before Whitten and his family were slated to acquire the whole building on Lispenard Street, there was a terrible fire. The setback was devastating, and Whitten and his family had to live in the studio on Crosby Street while he repaired and renovated the building on Lispenard himself. "I give thanks to God for knowing how to do construction," he said in a note dated January 31, 1983. In the three years it took to rebuild, Whitten couldn't make any work, and the family did not go to Crete because every resource was put into the restoration. This hiatus also prompted Whitten's shift away from paintings made with the developer.

Whitten's final studio was located on a quiet street in Woodside, Queens, almost directly beneath train tracks, its entrance an unassuming red door. Inside was mostly quiet, with jazz playing softly much of the time; occasionally, a train would rattle above, causing the whole small world to vibrate.

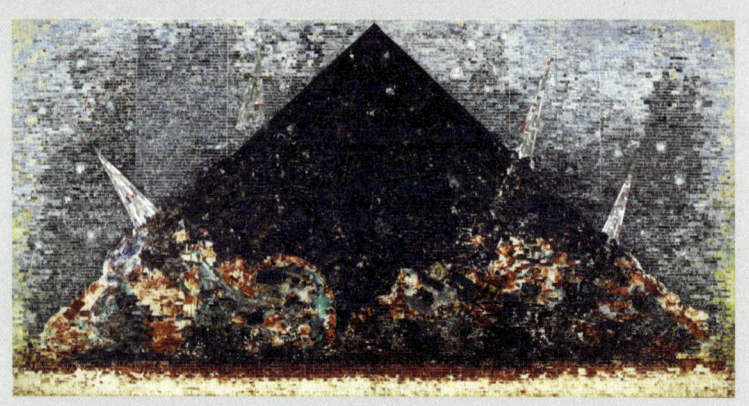

9.11.01, 2006
Acrylic and mixed media on canvas, 120 × 240 in. (304.8 × 609.6 cm)

One morning, standing on the street in front of the Lispenard Street building, Whitten heard a horrible sound. It was an airplane flying exceptionally low, and it crashed right into 1 World Trade Center, less than a mile south. This was, of course, September 11, 2001—a day Whitten could never shake from his memory. Having moved to TriBeCa in 1962, he knew the neighborhood before the giant towers. He had witnessed their construction and now he watched them be destroyed. Five years later, after his move to Woodside, he finished one of his most important paintings: *9.11.01*. It featured a large pyramid dividing the canvas into three triangles, with the base in flames and turning to rubble as the sky above it darkens. "The painting 9.11.01 is a promise to all those people murdered," Whitten wrote in his notes. "My objective in this painting is to put their suffering in paint. This is my job + I owe it to all those poor people."

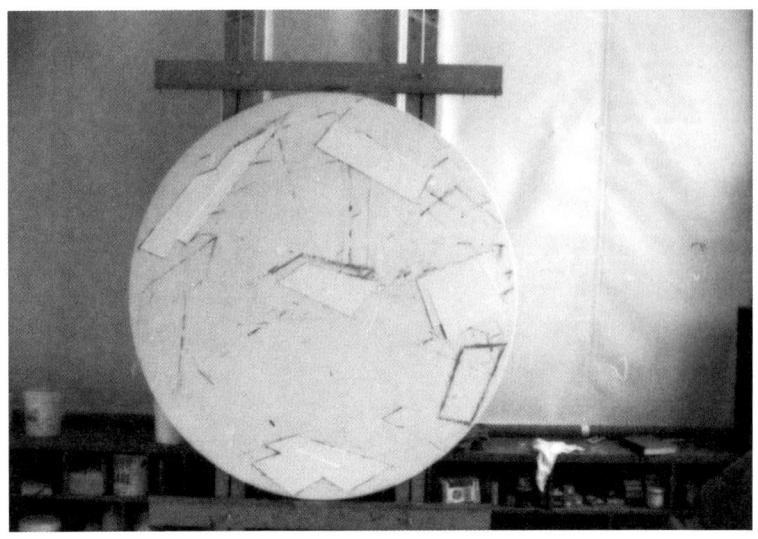

Whitten's Lispenard Street studio, New York, ca. 1980s

Whitten's studios were shrines in the literal sense of the word. Hanging in one corner of the studio in Woodside (p. 77)—and present in prior studios, including the one on Broome Street (p. 69)—was a large wooden effigy called *The Black Christ* that he had sculpted in 1967. A crown of thorns made from pointy sticks and nails adorned figure's head, and in its final form, fishbones covered its length, a sea of skeletons piled up at its base, the entire assemblage installed on top of a microwave. When Whitten arrived at the studio in the morning, he would light a candle, ring a bell with a curved wooden handle, and dab the effigy with olive oil (sourced from trees on his property in Crete) before he began to work. In the evening, he would ring the bell again, signaling the end of work for the day. This practice resonates with the West African tradition of paying homage to the gods at domestic shrines, where family members offer prayers and pour out libations to honor

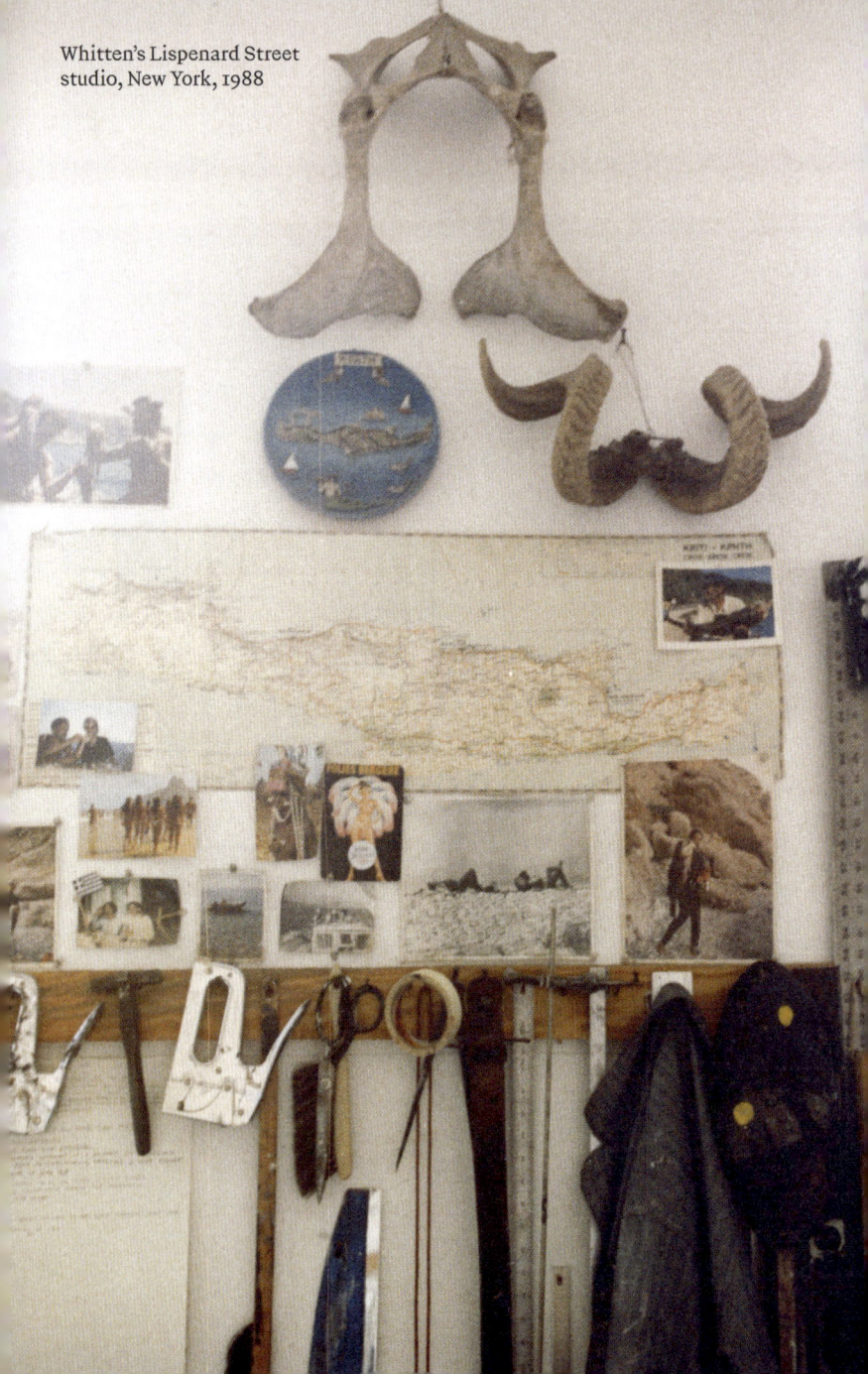

Whitten's Lispenard Street
studio, New York, 1988

ancestors during ceremonies, when seeking guidance, and even during everyday conversations. Whitten's personal ritual suggests he considered himself part of a long lineage, whose members he may have invited into the room every time he worked.

Whitten's studio was also a shrine in a broader sense, celebrating his life and his world. The studio walls were filled with important mementos: posters, newspaper clippings, photographs, strips of fabric, an axe, a dried rose, license plates, strings, masks, sculptures, and maps, all collected over decades. Many artists work with found materials, forming them into sculptures, but Whitten's relationship to this activity went deeper. Even in his private life he accrued these things, little bits piling on top of each other until they formed great mounds. Whitten's practice of collecting helps us see his paintings in a new light, as themselves accretions of materials like tesserae. Perhaps he saw the world as essentially fractal, composed of far-flung pieces that belonged together and which, with his work, he could reassemble into something new.

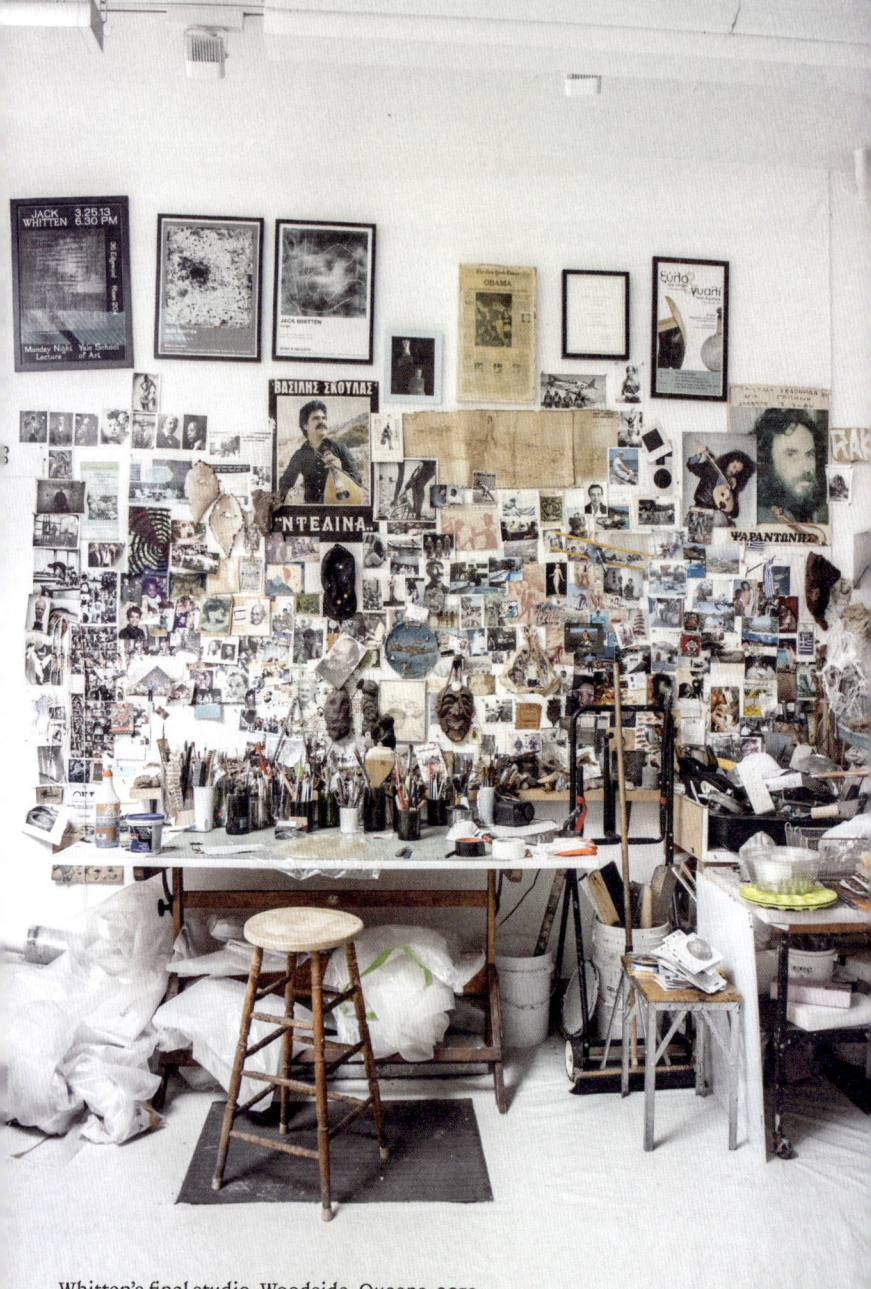

Whitten's final studio, Woodside, Queens, 2019

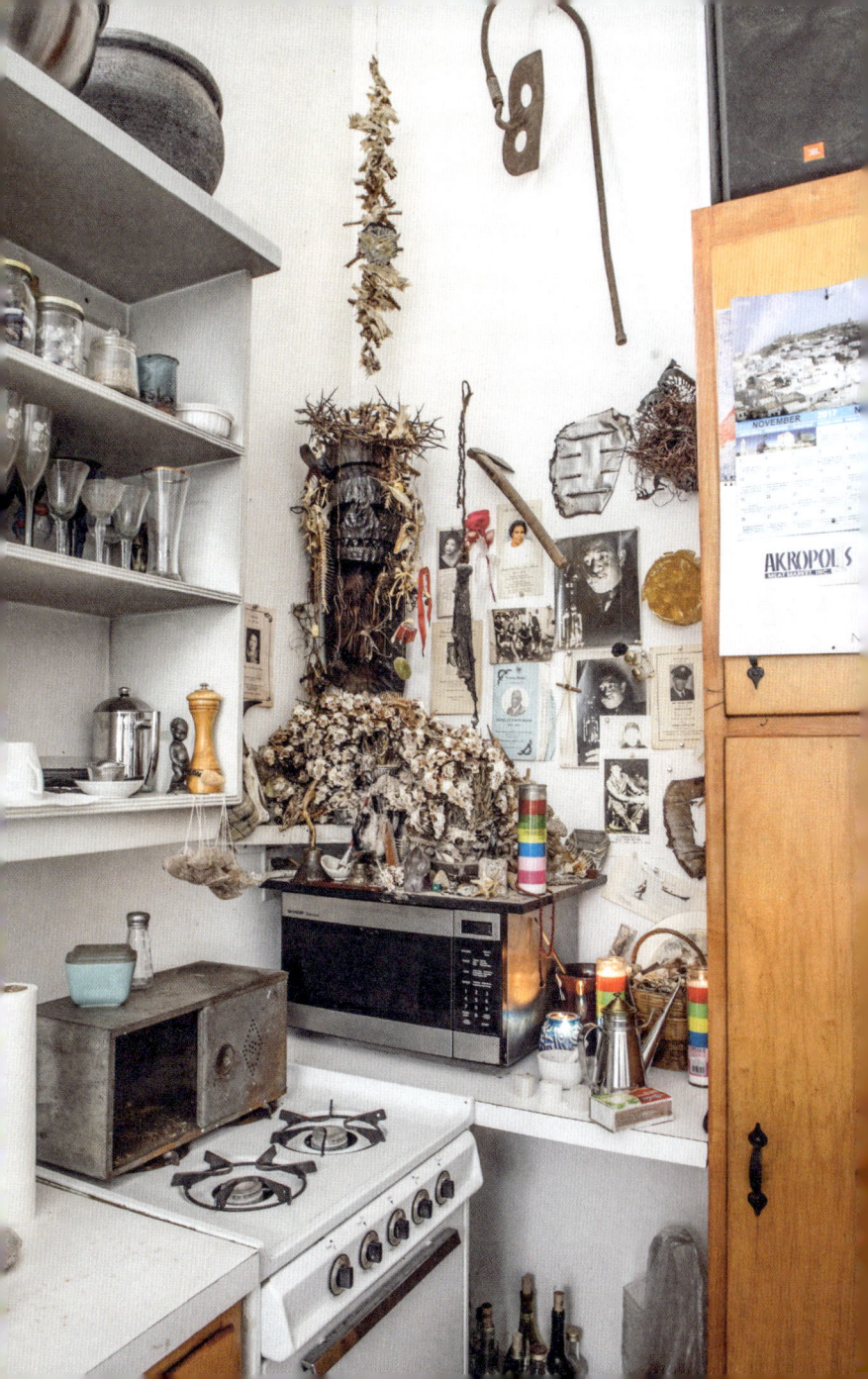

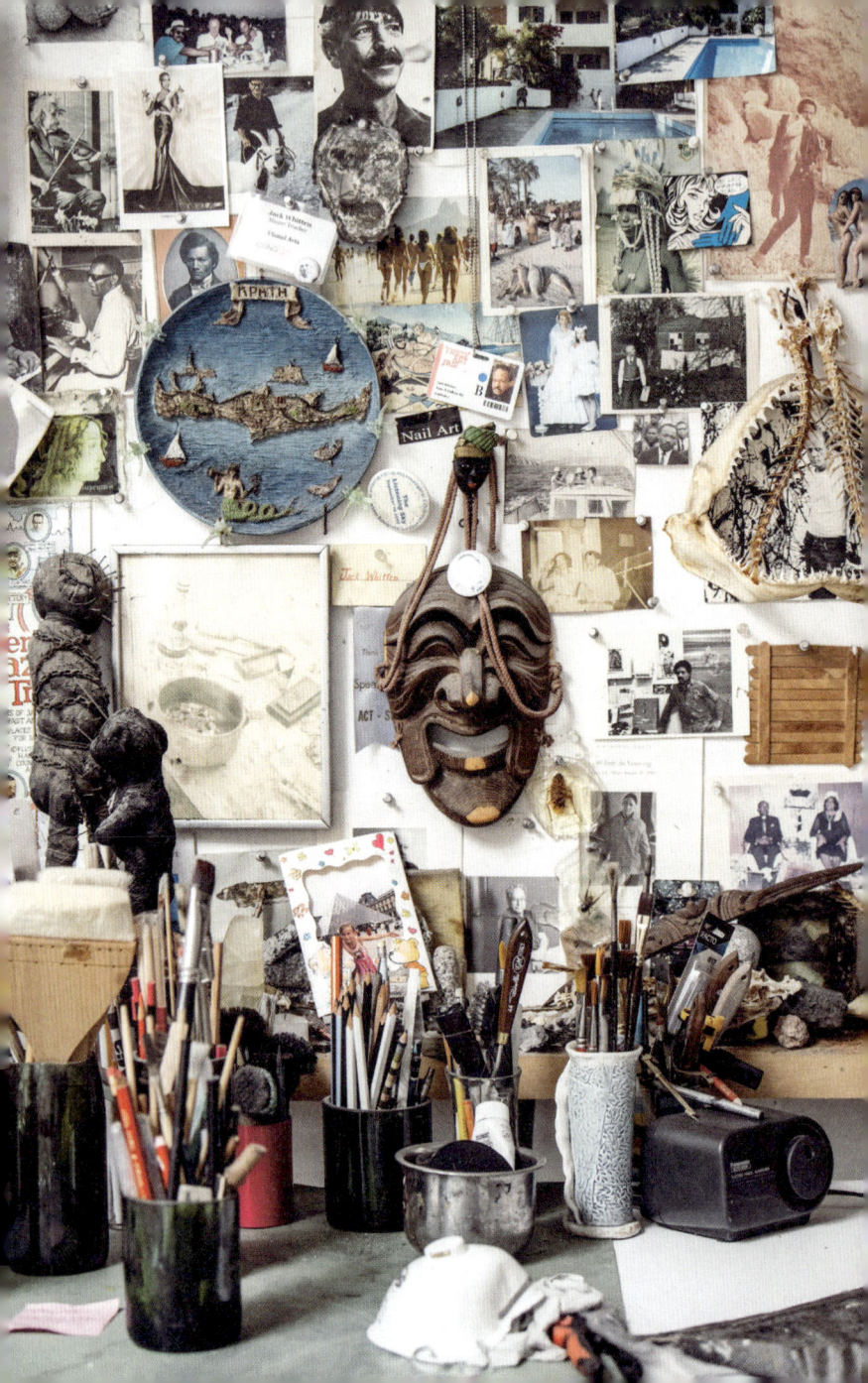

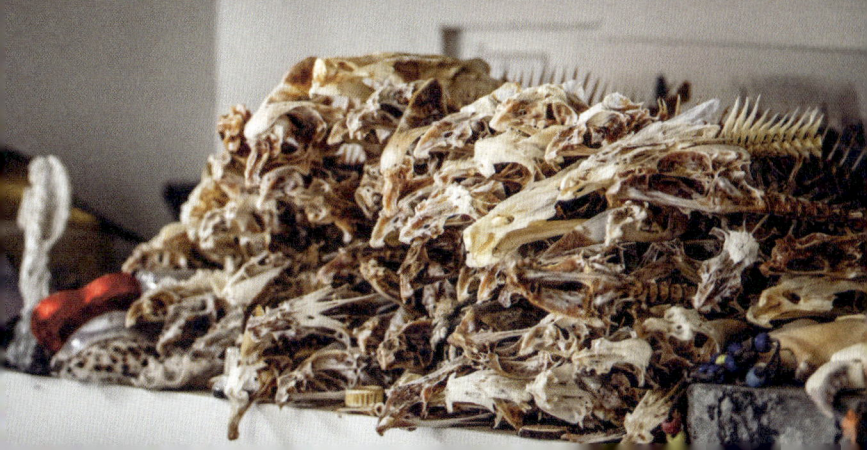

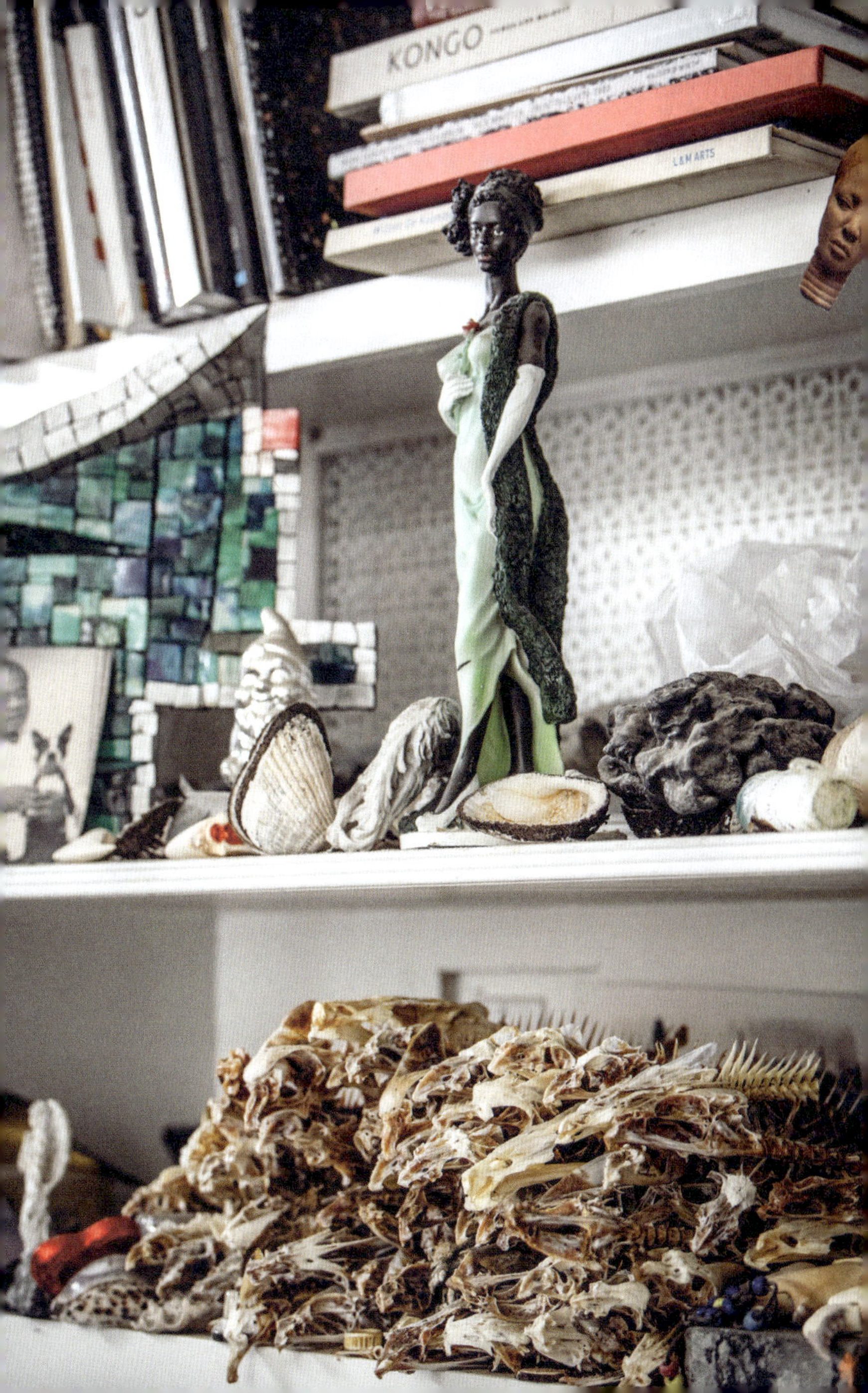

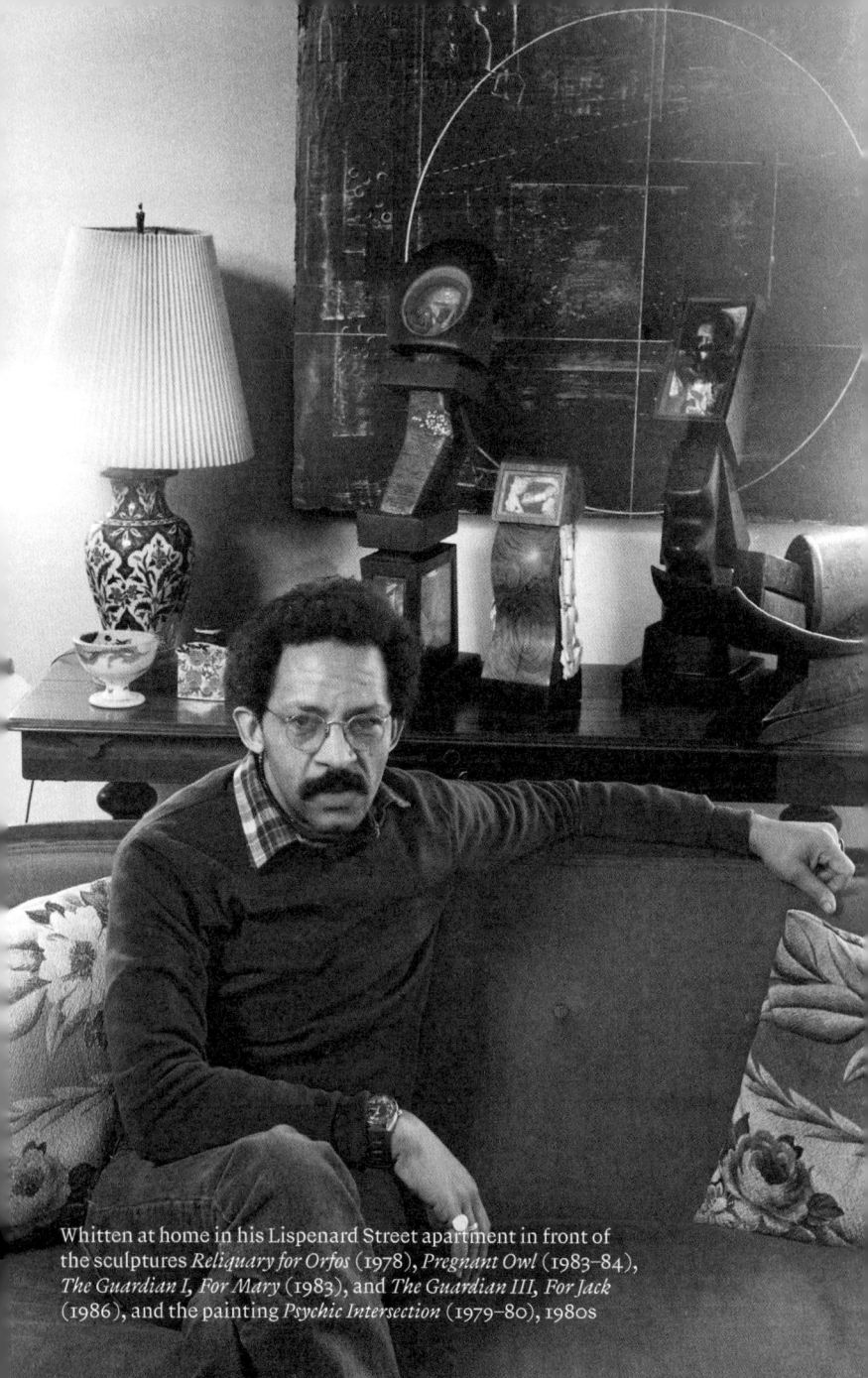

Whitten at home in his Lispenard Street apartment in front of the sculptures *Reliquary for Orfos* (1978), *Pregnant Owl* (1983–84), *The Guardian I, For Mary* (1983), and *The Guardian III, For Jack* (1986), and the painting *Psychic Intersection* (1979–80), 1980s

Elemental Matter

Whitten first encountered African sculpture during his summer trips to New York while still in school down south, visiting the Brooklyn Museum and the Metropolitan Museum of Art. He also encountered reproductions in books on African art. These sources offered some information—usually basic facts such as the objects' materials, the regions in which they were made and from which they were taken, as well as their social function—but they did so through an anthropological and colonialist lens that, for Whitten, prevented him from forming a connection with the sculptures. Nonetheless, he suspected that buried deep within African art was something that could help him as a young Black man living in the United States.

In fact, it was while looking closely at the work of modernist painters—especially the Cubists—that Whitten realized they had drawn inspiration from African art and consequently understood its substantial influence on the greatest European artists of the time. He recognized in the work of Picasso and Matisse what he called "formal sensations" derived from their study of African art's treatment of color, geometry, and surface. Yet Whitten felt there was something in these sculptures that the Cubists had failed to grasp, to penetrate.

In 1962 Whitten's friend and Cooper Union classmate Christopher Wilmarth (who later gained recognition for his glass works) loaned Whitten his first carving tools, and Leo Amino, Whitten's sculpture professor, known for his innovative work with plastic, helped him to begin thinking in three dimensions. But Whitten's interest in sculpture really took off when he met the

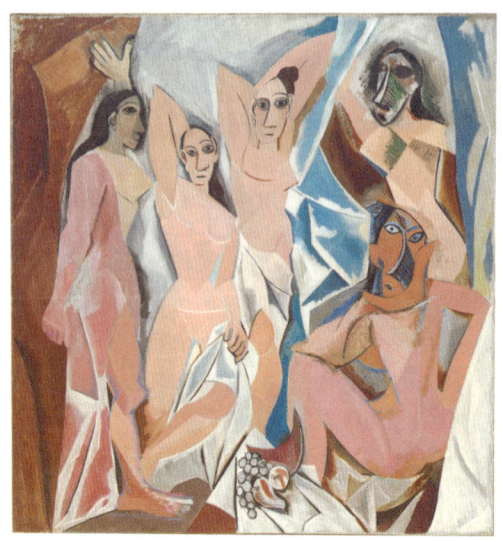

Pablo Picasso, *Les Demoiselles d'Avignon*, 1907.
Oil on canvas, 96 × 92 in. (243.9 × 233.7 cm)

dealer and collector Allan Stone in 1964. (Stone would
give Whitten his first solo exhibition at his eponymous
gallery in 1968.) Although known primarily as an expert
on Abstract Expressionism, Stone had eclectic taste, and
had built one of the largest private collections of African
art at the time. When he showed Whitten a work, he would
encourage him to "pick it up, feel it, smell it." These intense
and visceral encounters with the objects were pivotal for
Whitten. He came to consider wood "elemental matter,"
"waiting for someone to release its spirit," perhaps
believing this release was his job as an artist.

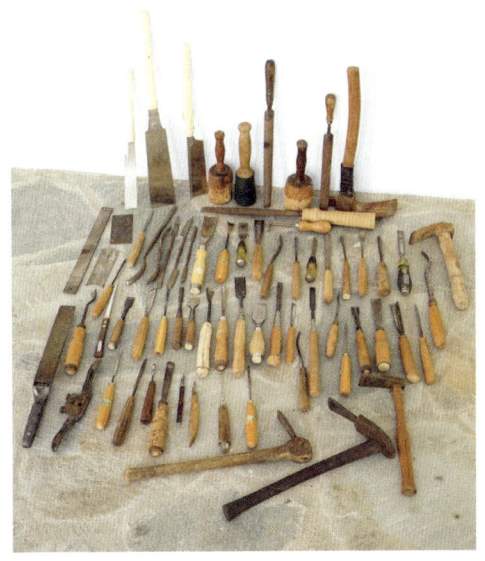

Whitten's sculpting tools, 2017

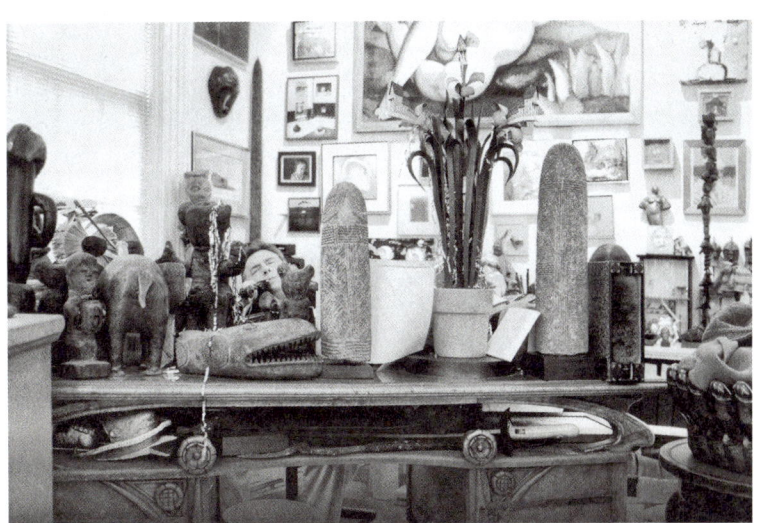

Whitten's first dealer, Allan Stone, with his art collection, 2001

Odyssey: Jack Whitten Sculpture, 1963–2017

Though Whitten first carved wood in the early 1960s,
and his practice flourished once he began regularly
spending summers in Crete starting in 1969, his
sculptures were seldom the focus of his exhibitions.
Many remained in Agia Galini simply because they were
too difficult to transport. Those that did make it back
to the United States were on display in Whitten's home
and shown only a handful of times in New York, so it was
not until *Odyssey: Jack Whitten Sculpture, 1963–2017*
that the broader public saw them for the first time.
The exhibition opened in April 2018, three months
after the artist's death, at the Baltimore Museum of
Art, then traveled to the Metropolitan Museum of Art,
New York. Years in the making, *Odyssey* was strongly
shaped by Whitten, as was its catalogue, which included
an essay he wrote, "Why Do I Carve Wood?," as well as
an autobiographical chronology. The exhibition included
forty sculptures and a selection of eighteen paintings—all
of his *Black Monoliths* series, among other works—as well
as Greek and African artifacts that provided art historical
context. Reviewing the show in the *New York Times*,
critic Roberta Smith described it as an "extraordinary
journey in three dimensions through art, culture,
time and personal experience."

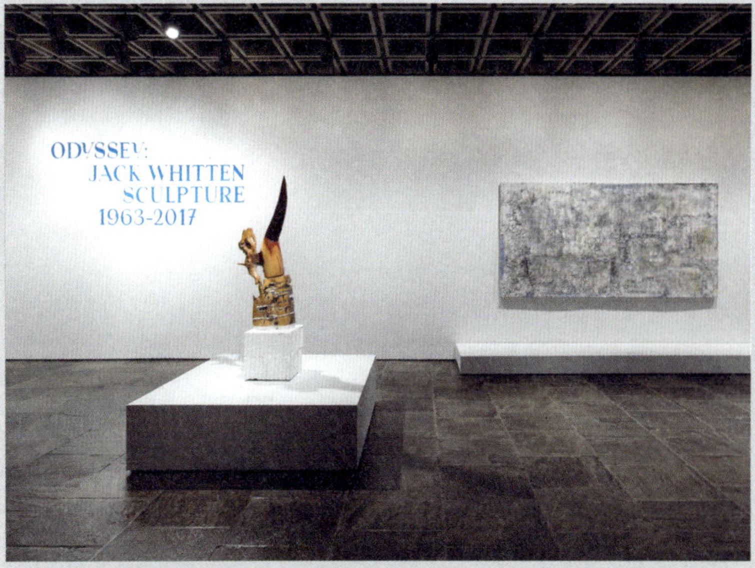

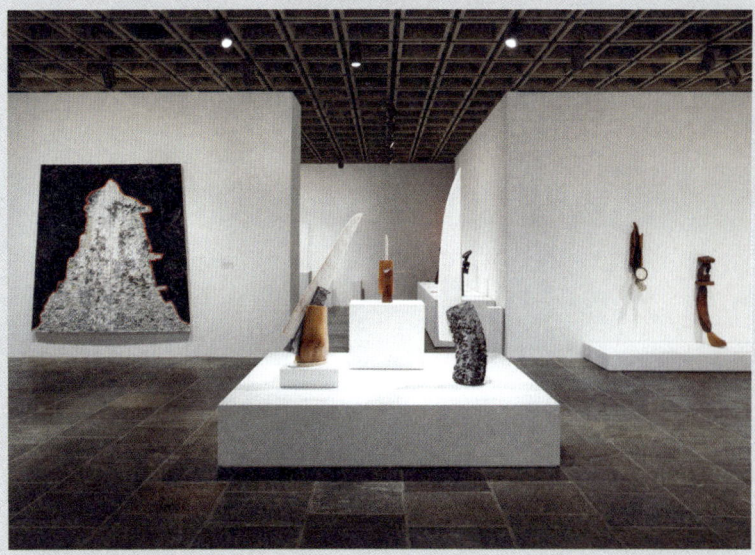

Installation views, *Odyssey: Jack Whitten Sculpture, 1963–2017*, Metropolitan Museum of Art, New York

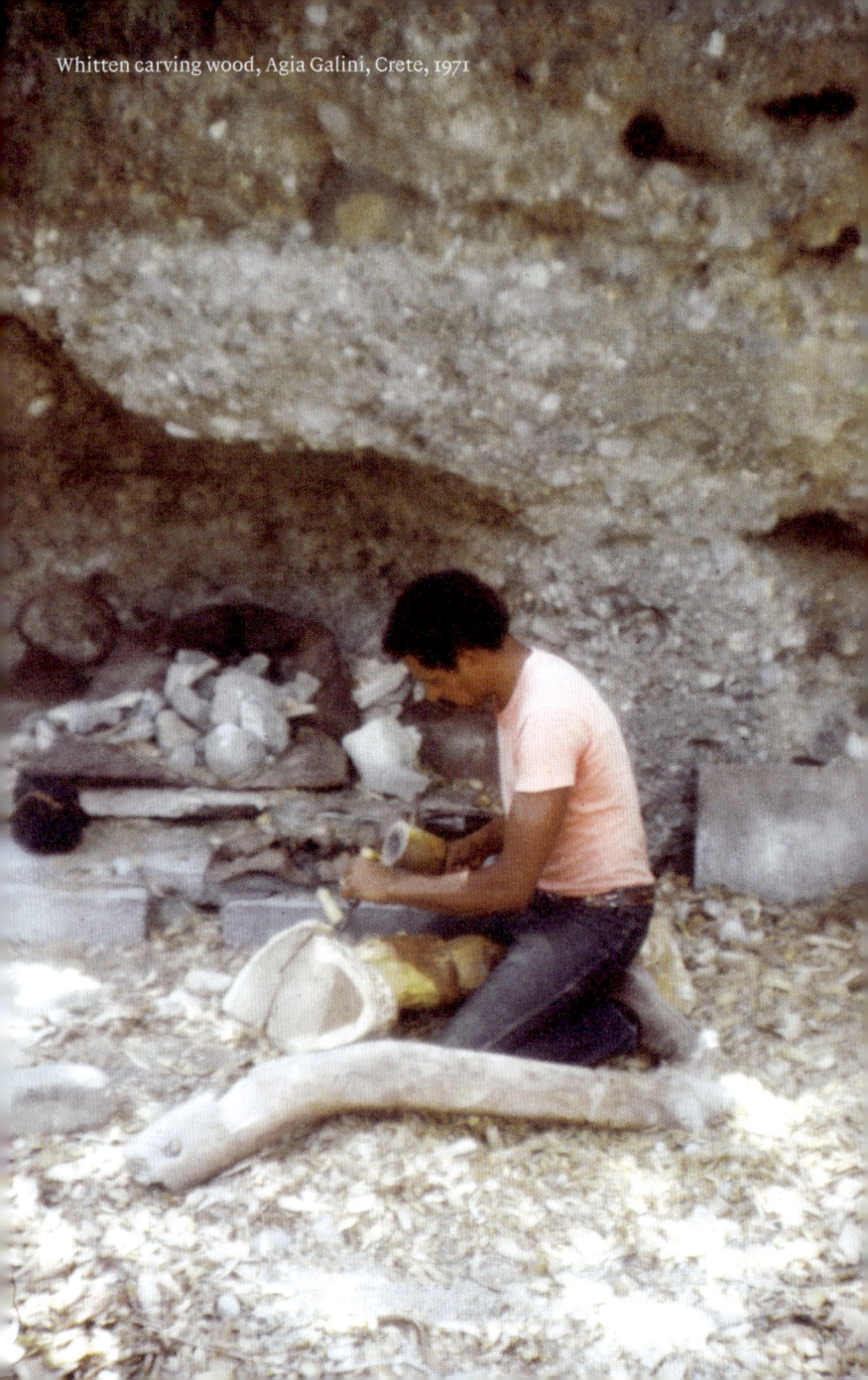

Whitten carving wood, Agia Galini, Crete, 1971

"When You Go to Greece You Are to Pack Your Carving Tools"

In a photograph of Whitten at work on a log, a rock fills the background, its rough surface mimicking the thousands of wood scraps on the floor. Whitten holds a mallet in one hand, a chisel in the other, his pink shirt glowing softly. The wood pressed between his thighs is partly finished, the unworked half looking dead and dry, the carved half appearing alive. Whitten nearly always worked this way when he carved wood: on his knees, outside, on the island of Crete, only in the summer. He enjoyed the physicality of the activity, with its lifting, hammering, and chopping; he loved the fresh air and the natural light; and he looked forward to showering outdoors after being covered in sweat and sawdust.

After Whitten began carving in Crete, he worked exclusively with wood—mostly walnut and black mulberry—from trees that grew on the island. He often discovered these logs by pure serendipity. Just before his first visit with his wife Mary to her familial homeland of Greece in summer 1969, Whitten had a dream. As he described it, "I saw a tree standing in a clearing. The dream said, 'When you go to Greece you are to pack your carving tools with you, find this tree, and carve it into a totem.' Freaky dream." He and Mary soon ran out of money in Athens and, following the advice of friends there, moved on to Crete, where the cost of living was lower. It was in the small village of Agia Galini—which, at the time, did not have electricity—that the couple found the tree from Whitten's dream in the town's harbor.

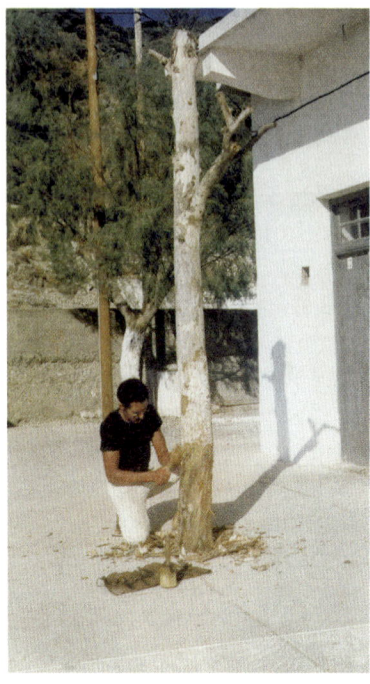

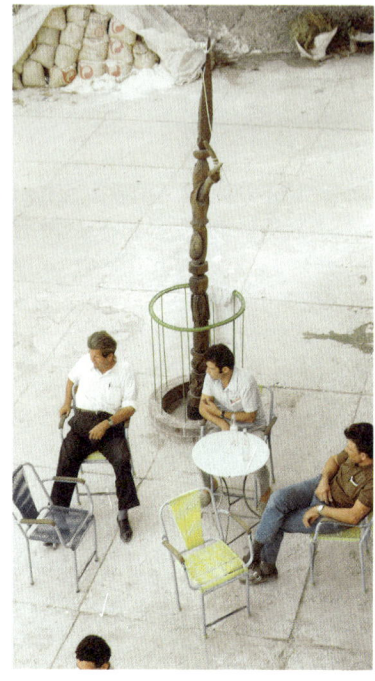

Whitten carving the tree that came to him in a dream, Agia Galini, Crete, 1969

The tree Whitten carved in Agia Galini, Crete, 1972

Whitten's influences are written all over his sculpture. Whereas in painting he sought to escape the prevailing style of the day, in sculpture he aimed to be in conversation with the past. Perhaps the most obvious example of this dynamic is *Ancestral Totem*, which he carved from the trunk of a birch tree in 1968. One of the few sculptures Whitten made in New York, *Ancestral Totem* set the tone for much of the work to follow. It features a stacked series of abstracted faces in the style of West African sculpture on a ten-foot-long pole. *The Saddle* (1977) also exemplifies his dialogue with African forms, displaying as it does attributes of the famous nineteenth-century *nkisi*, power figures originating from the Kongo peoples in what is today the Democratic Republic of Congo. The nkisi figures and *The Saddle* both bear on their surfaces agglutinations of smaller items—usually nails or fiber in the case of the former and diverse metallic components in the case of the latter.

Ancestral Totem, 1968. Birch wood, 121 × 14 × 7 in. (307.3 × 35.6 × 17.8 cm). Detail, p. 91

The Saddle, 1977. Cretan walnut, black mulberry, mixed media. 11 × 9 × 46 in. (27.9 × 22.9 × 116.8 cm). Detail, p. 90

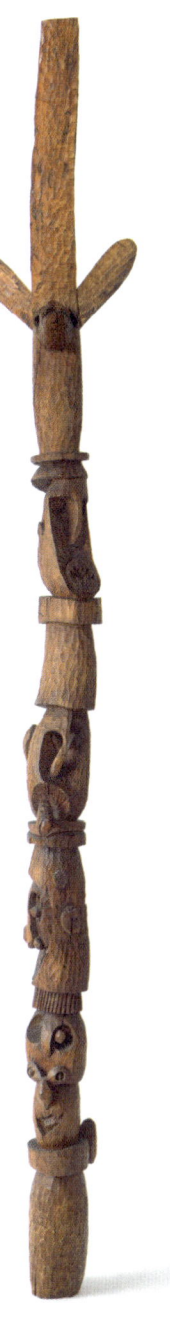

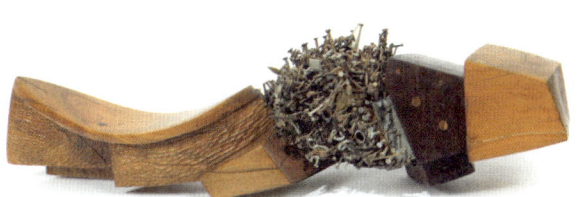

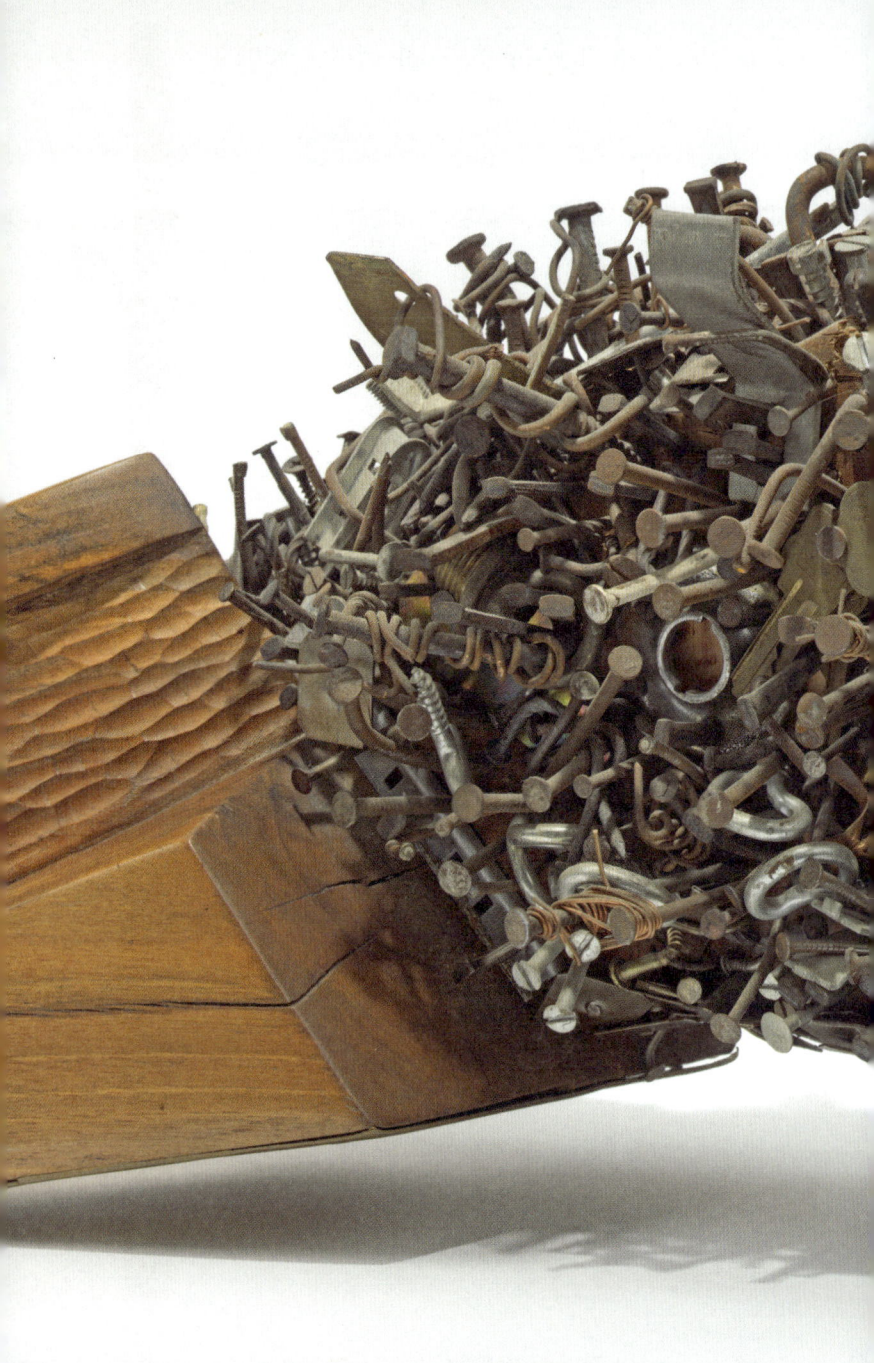

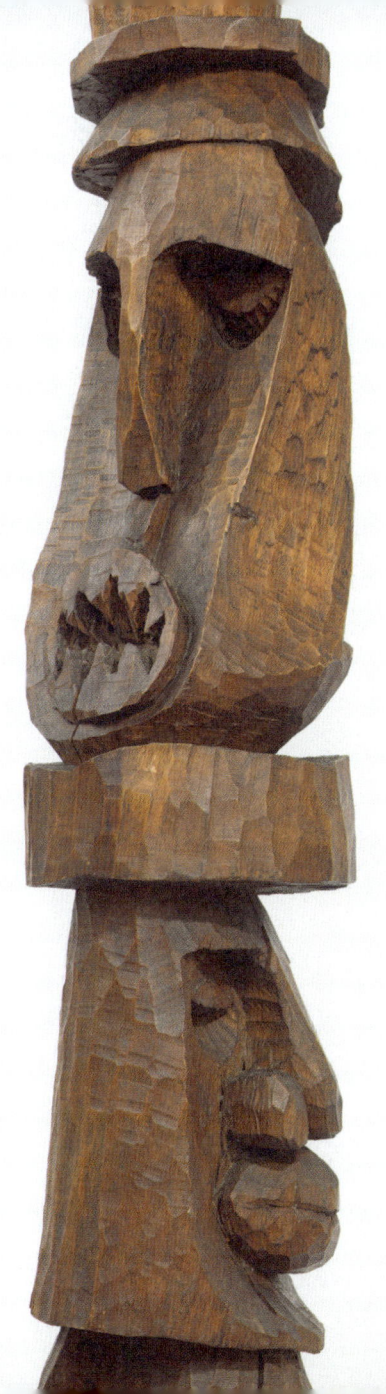

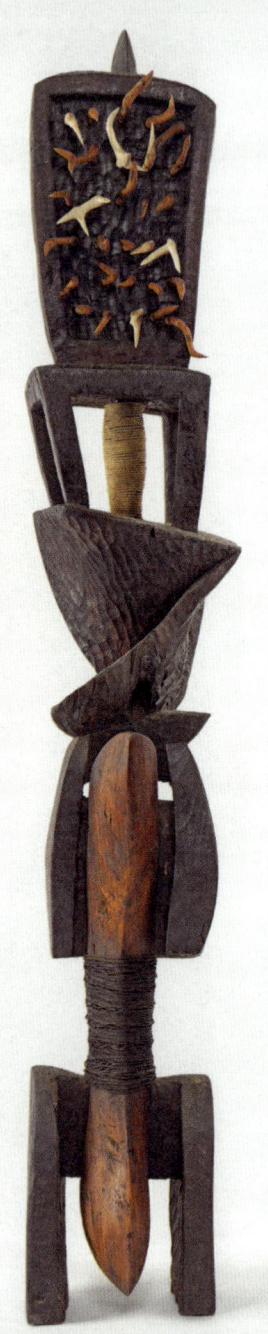

Anthropos #1, 1972.
Black and white mulberry,
wild olive wood, linen twine,
wire, 64⅛ × 9⅞ × 9⅞ in.
(162 × 25 × 25 cm)

"I have been carving wood since 1962. My carvings have definitely influenced my paintings.... The whole concept of making a painting as opposed to painting a painting came from my carving wood."

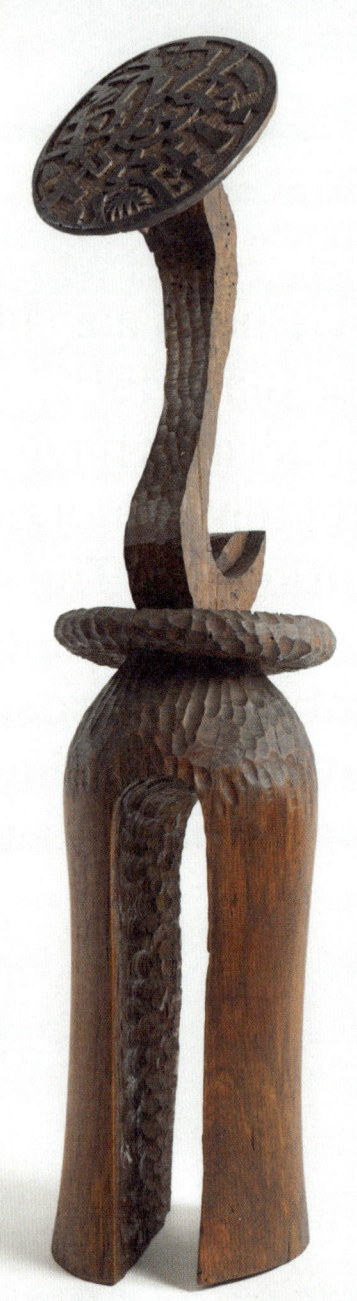

Sphinx, 1966–67.
Butternut wood,
36 × 10 × 10 in.
(91.4 × 25.4 × 25.4 cm)

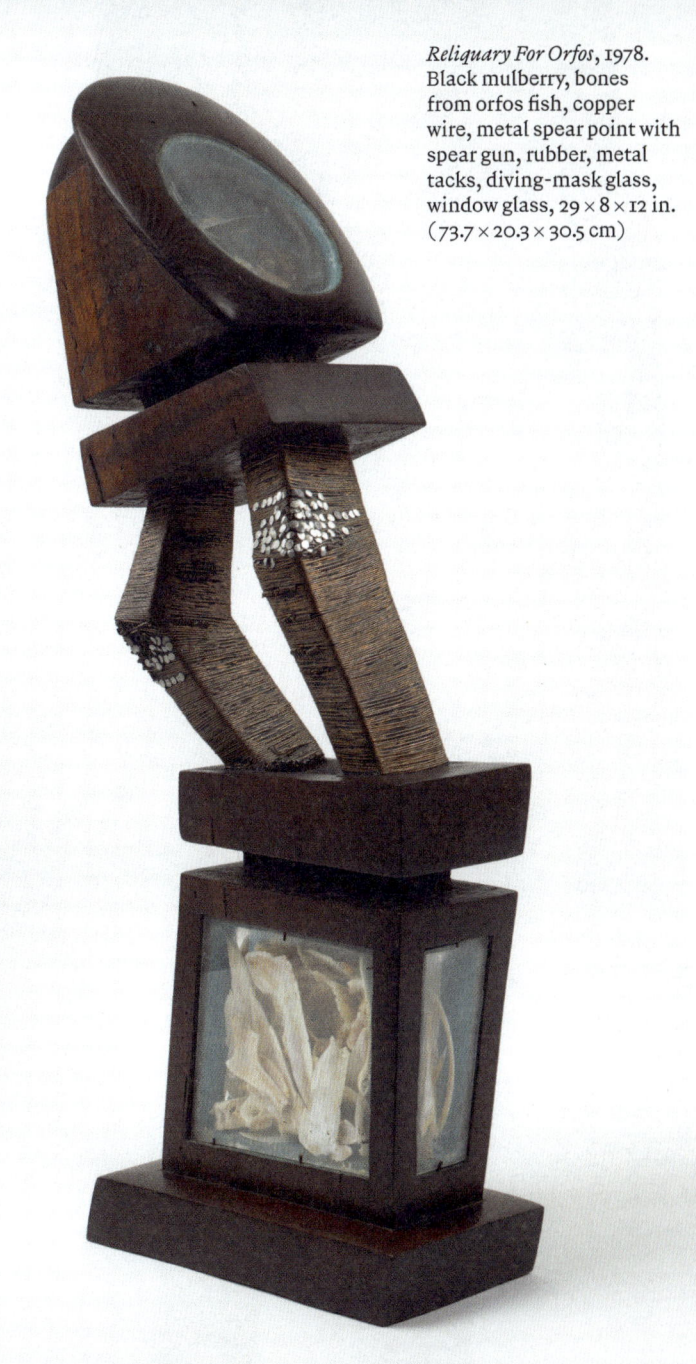

Reliquary For Orfos, 1978.
Black mulberry, bones
from orfos fish, copper
wire, metal spear point with
spear gun, rubber, metal
tacks, diving-mask glass,
window glass, 29 × 8 × 12 in.
(73.7 × 20.3 × 30.5 cm)

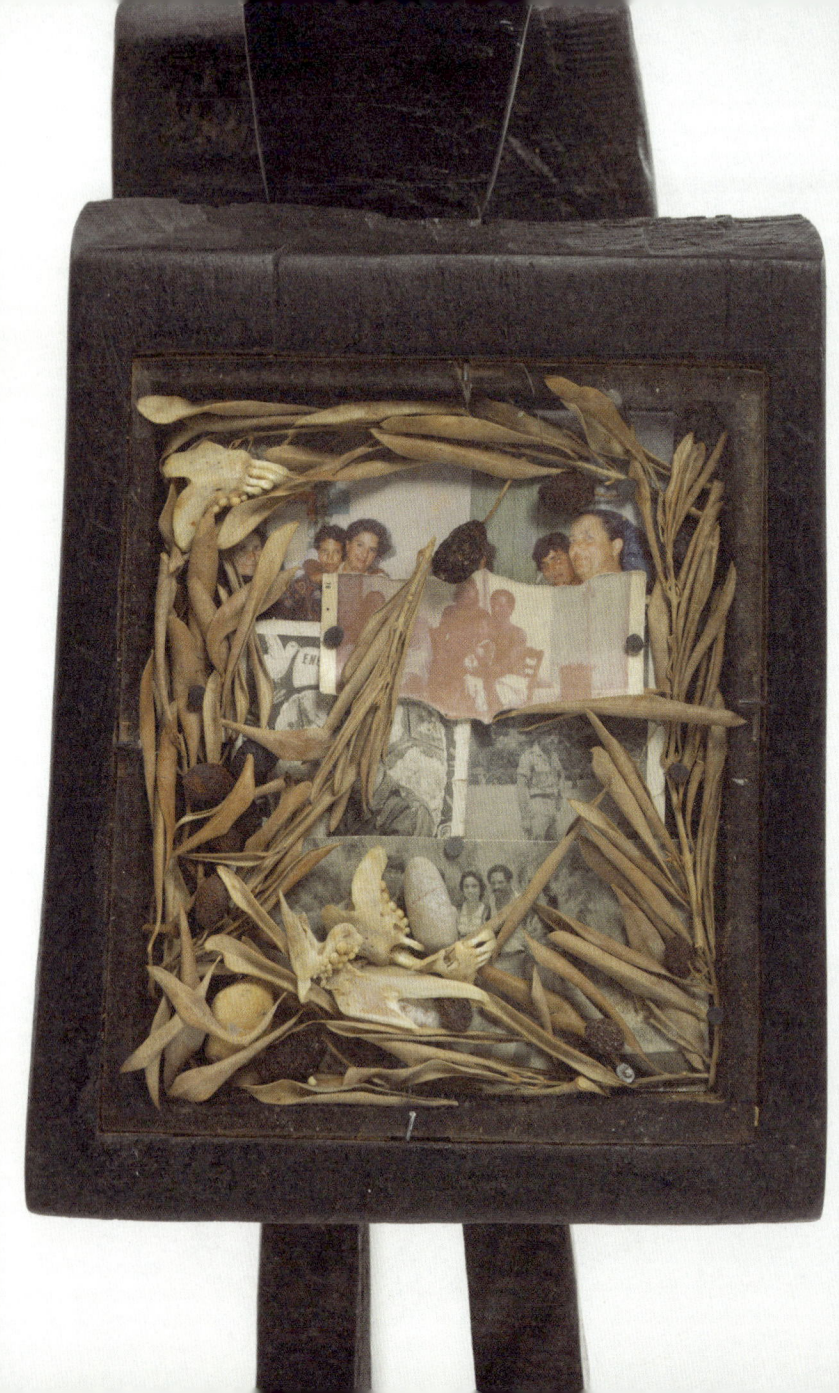

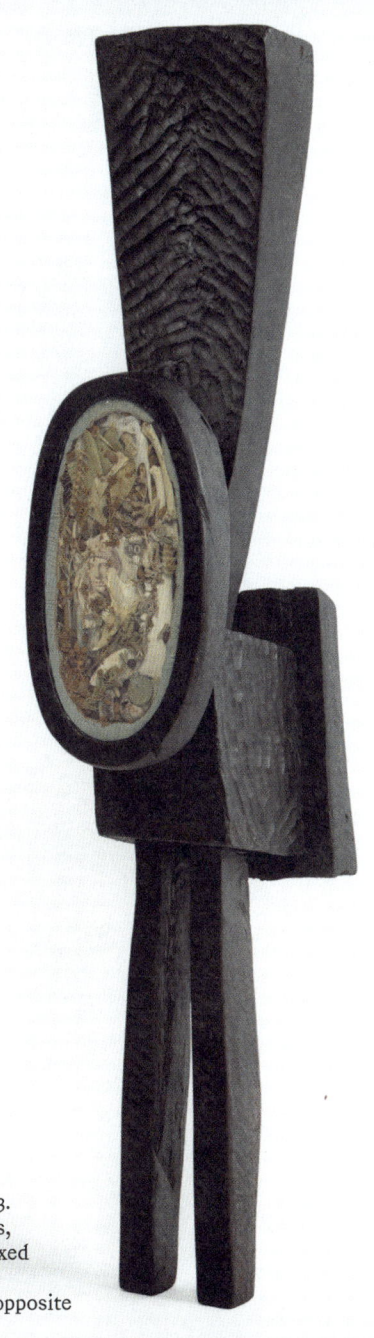

Memory Container, 1972–73.
Black mulberry, fish bones,
seashells, linen twine, mixed
media, 42⅛ × 8¼ × 8⅝ in.
(107 × 21 × 22 cm). Detail opposite

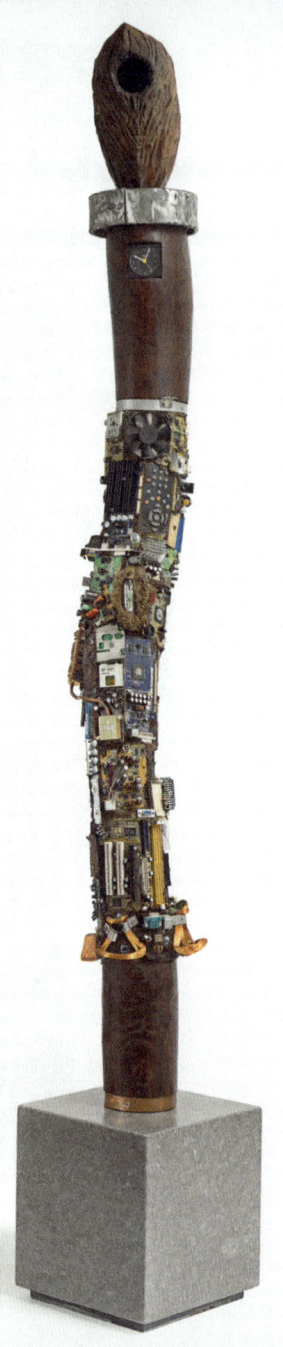

Technological Totem Pole, 2013.
Black mulberry, mixed media,
metal, Gortynis marble, Braun
alarm clock, 82⅝ × 11¾ × 11¾ in.
(210 × 30 × 30 cm). Detail opposite

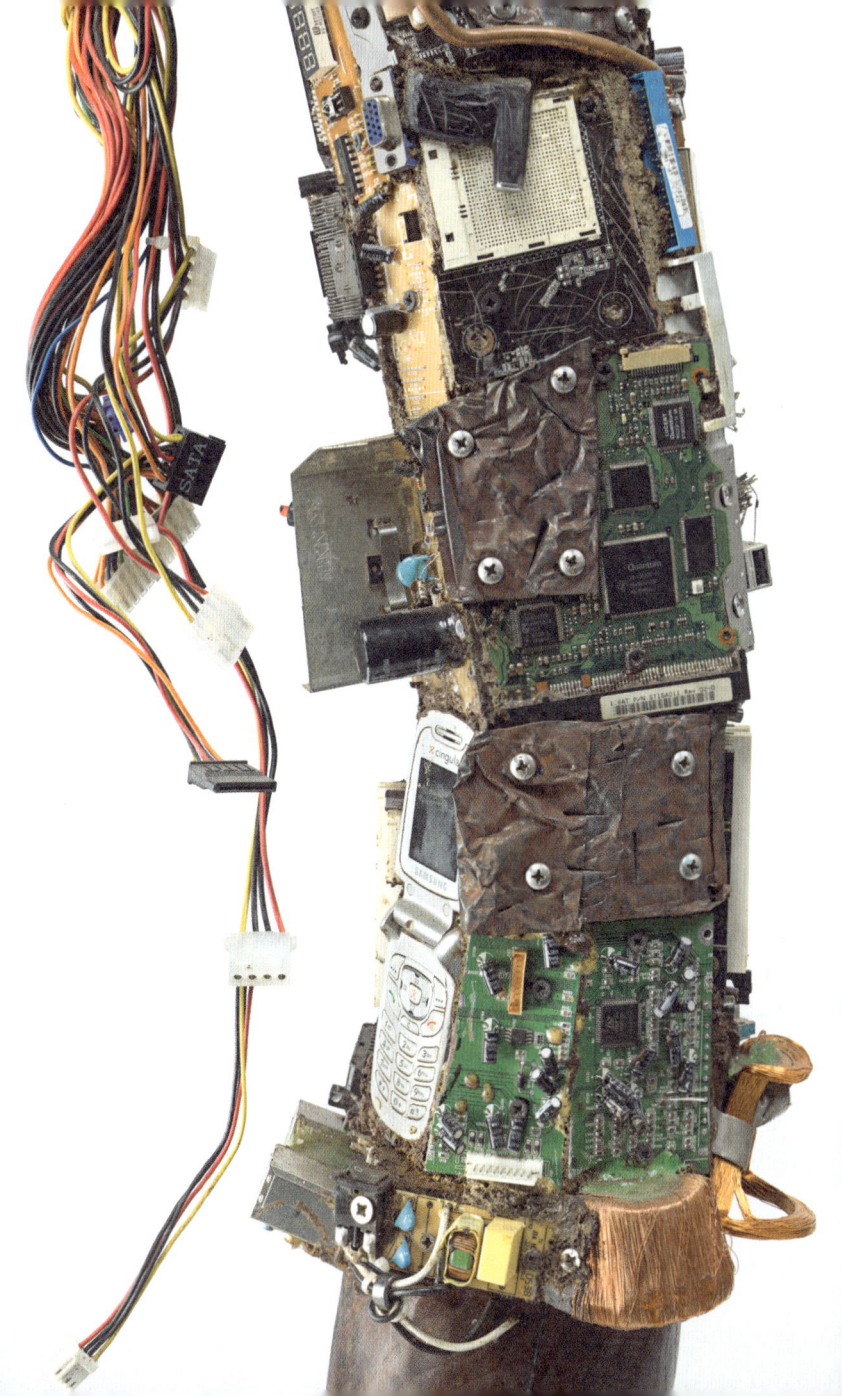

The Guardians

Today, many collectors are drawn to African sculpture for its beauty, but in its original context, it performed a very different function. Among the Yoruba, sculpture is central to domestic shrines. When a child was born, the parents would consult an oracle to know which god was compatible with the child's destiny; the child would be dedicated to that god, and a shrine would be erected in the home for the child to converse with their guardian. Among the Igbo, *ikenga*—typically small carved wooden figures with human faces and sometimes animal features such as horns—were kept in the home, representing an embodiment of an individual's *chi*, or personal god, and signifying their strength. Ikenga are deeply revered and sacred, so destroying another person's ikenga was, historically, tantamount to a declaration of war, as shown in Chinua Achebe's 1964 novel *Arrow of God*.

Was Whitten thinking about these things when he began to carve "guardians" dedicated to his family members? He made one for his wife Mary, one for his daughter Mirsini, and one for himself. Whitten's versions abstracted the human features typically found on ikenga and other African sculpture, but their shapes remain affective, and we can still recognize the spiritual force behind the intent with which they were made. The last in the set— *The Guardian III, For Jack* (1986)—differs greatly from *The Guardian I, For Mary*, made three years earlier. Mary's sculpture has curves, perhaps depicting feminine energy, and a compartment at the top that holds objects including locks of her hair, bus tickets, and olive leaves from Agia Galini. Whitten's is more muscular, with three distinct components that resemble a shield, a saddle, and a knife.

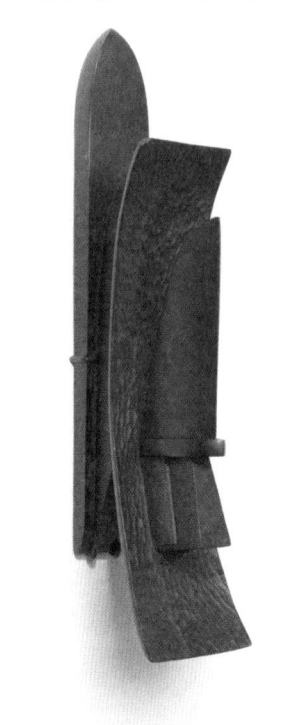

The Guardian III, For Jack, 1986.
Black mulberry and nylon fishing line,
34½ × 7 × 12 in. (87.6 × 17.8 × 30.5 cm)

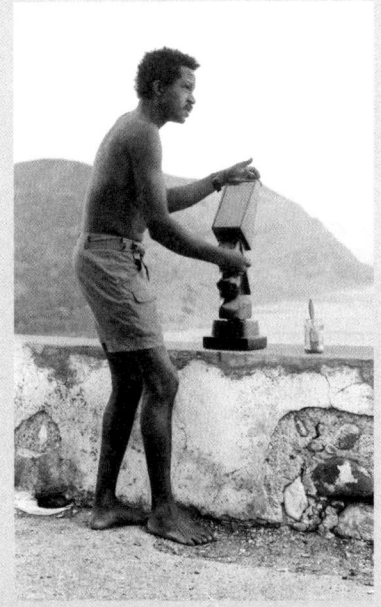

Whitten with *The Guardian I, For Mary* (1983), Agia Galini, Crete, ca. 1983

101

STUDIO LOG '96

+FRIEND

14 DEC: COMPLETED THE MINGO ALTERPIECE : FOR MY STUDENT GEORGE MINGO
                                                    ^

18 DEC: I AM A PART OF NATURE.

SPIRIT

2 ♦ DEC : I revisited the grid today. Painting is like riding a comet, she swings way out
on an orbit & returns. My job is to stay on top! The 'broken grid series' was fun
with a lot of freedom & very romantic but let's face it everything is gridded.
I plan to start a series of bold black & white, 'Revisited GRID SERIES', Digital
Abstraction Part II. Since Franz Kline is more & more important to me,
even more so than De Kooning, I will dedicate this series to Franz.
Also, I have been thinking about the Formal ..... the Formal could be conceived
of as 'Personal Myth'. This notion of the Formal attracts me very much.
I shall try to penetrate this notion with the 'Revisited Grid Series'
    ✱ FIRST ONE IS TO BILL

This is what my
subject is.
7 Jan 97

1997

7 JAN: THE UNIVERSE IS NOT CASUAL.

8 JAN: SPIRIT
         ⟩ THIS ALLOWS ME TO RECONSTRUCT REALITY.
MATTER ── ENERGY

14 JAN: BLACK AESTHETICS IS ALL INCLUSIVE. (NOT TO BE CONFUSED WITH SO CALLED "BLACK ART")

16 JAN: AT SOME POINT IN LIFE, ONE MUST STOP CHASING & LET IT COME TO YOU.

25 JAN: IT'S THE THIRD ENTITY THAT I WANT.

31 JAN: I AM A HISTORICAL FACT.

20 MARCH: ABSTRACTION IS THE ESSENCE OF BEING.

22 MARCH: IS THERE AN ABSTRACT REALISM?

27 MARCH: THE DRAWING IS A CATALYST.

1 APRIL : THE PHILOSOPHY OF JAZZ IS THE EXPANSION OF FREEDOM, FROM INSIDE → OUT
    OUT IS ALWAYS EXPANDING THE PARAMETERS OF FREEDOM. JAZZ IS ALL INCLUSIVE.

10 APRIL: YES GOD ! BRIGHT MOMENTS, 1995 FOR RASAN ROLAND KIRK
    THE PAINTING IS AN EXTENSION OF NATURE ; THEREFORE I AM A MEGACEPTUALIST

14 APRIL: I WANT THAT WHICH IS A MATTER OF FACT.

15 APRIL: COMPLETED THE GREAT WHITE : FOR BILL DE KOONING   1430 HRS.

6 MAY: MY PAINTING PROCESS IS NOT LABOR INTENSIVE IT'S LOVE INTENSIVE.

7 MAY: COMPLETED THE GINSBURG MANDALA : FOR ALLEN GINSBURG

17 MAY : I AM A DIGITAL EXPRESSIONIST.

22 MAY: GONE FISHING

see you in Sept

Whitten's studio notes, December 14, 1996, to May 22, 1997

Woodshedding:
Whitten's Writing

While we most often have to infer artists' creative processes from their work, interpreting and attributing our own meanings to their visual language, many artists have given us more direct access to their thinking via their writings— from treatises meant for public consumption to private journals and diaries. Idiosyncratic and personal as these latter texts may be, they nonetheless can constitute great literary achievements.

In Whitten's case, we have notes that he kept from 1962 to the end of his life. The entries are clearly dated, making their chronology easy to follow. He often wrote in a stream of consciousness, and frequently in all uppercase letters. On some days—especially in the sections labeled "Studio Logs"—he recorded only a single sentence. On other days he wrote many pages. Some of the entries resemble poetry, with line breaks and spaces between stanza-like sections, while others run on without interruption, like prose. Whatever the form, Whitten's words tend to move smoothly from theory to events in his personal life and back again— the two topics seemingly indistinguishable for him.

Whitten's notes demonstrate that he was a deeply inquisitive man, even—or especially—in private, contending with his preconceived notions and working hard to acquire fresh perceptions. (Indeed, "Notes from the Woodshed," the title he gave his studio logs from 2009 onwards, refers to the jazz musician's concept of "woodshedding," or practicing in private, free to experiment with ideas before taking them public.) A very early entry immediately pulls us into Whitten's deepest artistic concerns with its first line: "Objects do not exist without the presence of space as space is not ~~present~~ noticeable without objects." Whitten was just twenty-three when he wrote this statement, but he was already beginning to grapple with the thoughts that would preoccupy him his entire career.

Even as a young artist, Whitten was frank with himself and regarded no topic as off the table in his writing. His notes were a space where he could be vulnerable, where he could construct and reconstruct his own identity. An entry from June 24, 1964, interrogates what it means to be a man in the United States at the time: "Beneath every surface lies an identity," he wrote. "The amount of depth beneath the surface determines the value of its being. What is the depth of America in the year 1964? What is the depth of its people? Are the people able to see their face in the palm of their hands?"

On many days, Whitten simply logged what had happened in the studio, recording the process he had followed to get a painting done. Consider February 18, 1973: "I have made a full circle. I worked so hard to build my platform and giant 12' squeegee expecting to continue painting in the same manner by pulling across the surface." On other days, like March 25, 1973, he recorded a visit to (and judgement of) a place: "The trip to California was quite nice—lovely country but couldn't live there. I don't like California Culture."

In Whitten's notes, we also get to witness his private anxieties and disappointments. When he did not receive a Guggenheim Fellowship in 1974, he wrote, "I DID NOT GET THE GUGGENHEIM! This is a very low blow for me." It was not so much the prestige of the prize, but the money.

He continues, "I am broke not able to Paint, a one-show at the Whitney Museum in Sept, not real[l]y pleased with the paintings that I have—and no materials... " He also reported on the toll being an artist was taking on his mental health: "I have been so depressed that it has been almost a month since I've written anything or painted. An artist, without materials is like a junkie without his shit!"

Yet Whitten's notes also reveal his unbreakable spirit. On December 5, 1979, he wrote: "Today I am forty years old. I have three dollars in my pocket and after paying the rent a remaining of twelve dollars in my bank account. Keita needs a winter coat + shoes. I have been sick and owe money for doctor bills. Mary + I are trying to raise money in order to buy the Lispenard St. building. Further, Christmas is coming in three weeks. Do you think I am worried? NO! Of course I have no money. I am an artist, what do you expect? My work is evolving and getting stronger, I have my health, my family, a great wife, great kid and I must say with no strings attached we are happy and enjoying our life!"

"Battle Plan" and "Objectives"

Whitten rigorously chronicled the conceptual development of his painting practice, often jotting down the ideas with which he was wrangling as short aphorisms. Two of his more regimented, list-like studio logs are reproduced here as both facsimiles and transcripts: one, a "Battle Plan," begins in fall of 1983 and ends on March 29, 1984, and registers the development in his thinking over time; the other, a list of "Objectives," was written on October 8, 1998, demonstrating the robust certainty underlying his artmaking at a single moment in time. (In seeking to preserve Whitten's voice, the transcriptions of his writings in this book reproduce the spacing, punctuation, and spelling of the originals as faithfully as possible.)

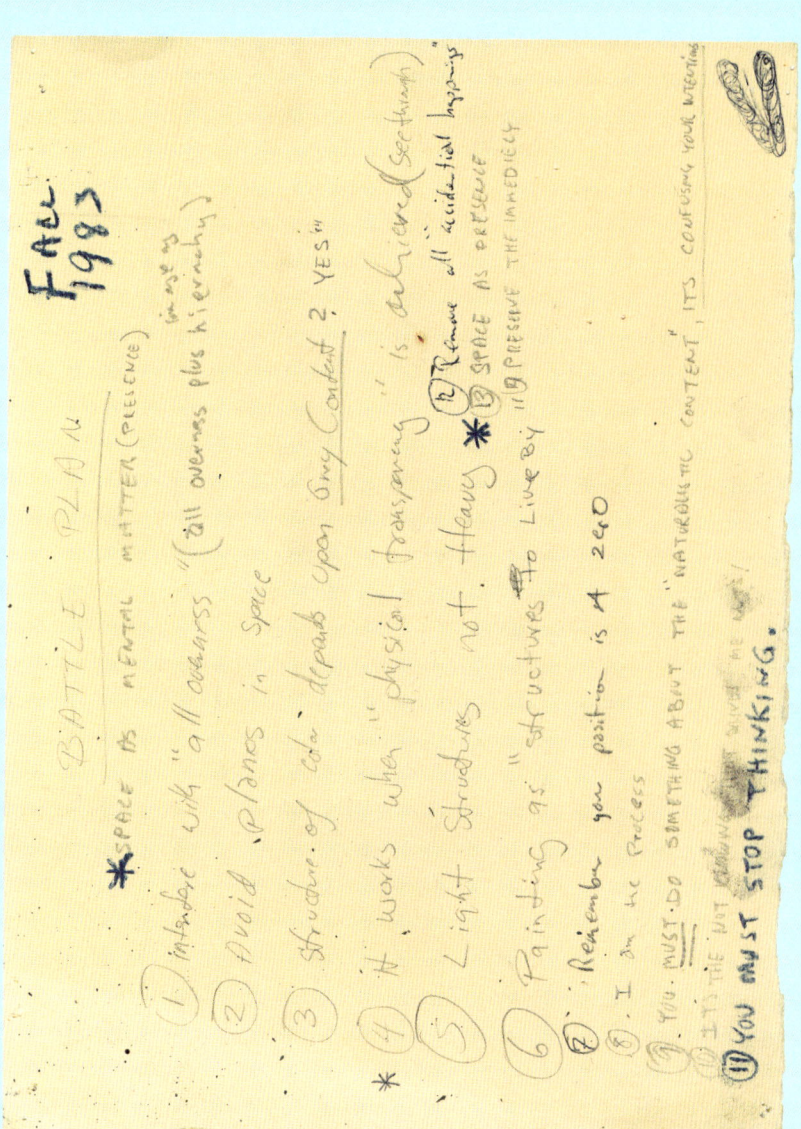

Whitten's "Battle Plan" from his studio notes, fall 1983 – March 29, 1984

The Artist's Voice

15. Painting as a spiritual act; a means of communicating with the spirit } 20 Dec 83

16. The technical device is a reminder of what I am not who I am

17. Geometry is only a vehicle an armature for getting there " I need some known value the intellect is good for this purpose (do research a fusion fault movement)

18. Great. ART must be able to go beyond the self

*19. Necessary to amplify. It works when the Spirit is present. Paintings become containers for the spirit, a place or object to contain the spirit. (25 DEC 83)

20. The process has always been one of transformation

21. Is there such an animal as Aesthetic Behavior?

22. Take the conceptual and crossbred it with pure spirituality.

23. All cultures defined in terms of 1 intrinsic value of its source being spiritual from within.

24. There is no definable formula

25. SPACE AIN'T NOTHING BUT TASTE!

26. The structure is trichotomy not dichotomy (my earlier interpretation was shortsighted of me.) } 24 Jan '84

27. Inner man + Outer space = SPIRIT

28. Am I addressing myself to a new vocabulary or simply taking the old and looking at it in another space?

29. I, what way is my perspective different from Renaissance perspective? } 9 FEB '84

30. Is I throw out masculinity, is I throw out objectuality, if I throw out ethnicity, what am I left with? — What risk are involved with them, life?

31. I do not want to orchestrate Art History.

32. A NEW SPACE, A NEW PLACE, A NEW RENAISSANCE — 10 FEB 84

16,81,90,91,29,3

33. The spirit is not conceptual Knowledge. 14 FEB 84

34. EMCA painting is a surprise!

35. I am not German. I have not committed any crimes against humanity. 16 FEB 84
My soul is not Portland.

36. Each painting is legend. 17 FEB 84

37. There is madness out there + somebody's got to do something about it. 27 FEB 84
I am an ENERGY FIELD PAINTER. 28 FEB 84

38.

39. I am more interested in what lies color leaves behind; its tracks. 3 March

40. II AM LOOKING FOR SOMETHING TO BASE MY LIFE UPON, A BELIEF SYSTEM.
AN ARTISAN FOR LIVING. 6 MARCH

41. It's the first I come out of the closet. No large can I? Yanni Brotherness...

42. I use the energy field to produce magic objects + each one must be
different from the other. 12 March 84

43. MAYBE EVERYTHING THAN ARTIST'S SAY IS BALONEY! 15 March (old substantial baloney)

44. I am a carver of light. 19 March

45. Sometimes I feel as if I am trying to steal western civilization. 22 March

46. FREE THE SOCIETY!

47. The plane is no substitute for the week. 27 March 84

46. The presence that I speak of is something spiritual and it exist in space. 27 March 84

47. Maybe that Joseph Campbell is right. Society is always in need of myth. Could my
works do all that? 29 March

BATTLE PLAN
*SPACE AS MENTAL MATTER (PRESENCE)

1. interfere with "all overness" (all overness plus image as hierarchy)
2. Avoid planes in space
3. structure of color depends upon <u>Gray Content</u>? YES'84
*4. it works when "physical transparency" is achieved (see through)
5. Light Structures not Heavy
6. Painting as "structures" to Live By"
7. Remember your position is at zero
8. I am the Process
9. YOU <u>MUST</u> DO SOMETHING ABOUT THE "NATURALISTIC CONTENT", <u>ITS CONFUSING YOUR INTENTIONS</u>
10. IT'S THE NOT KNOWING THAT DRIVES ME NUTS!
11. YOU MUST STOP THINKING.
12. Remove all "accidental happenings"
*13. SPACE AS PRESENCE
14. PRESERVE THE IMMEDIECY
15. Painting as a spiritual act; a means of communicating with the spirit
16. The technical device is a <u>reminder</u> of <u>where I am</u> not who I am

} 20 Dec. 83

17. Geometry is only a vehicle an armature for getting "there," I need some known value, the intellect is good for this purpose (do research on Russian const. movement)
18. Great ART must be able to get beyond the self
*19. Necessary to modify: It works when the Spirit is present. Paintings become containers for the spirit, a place or object to contain the spirit. (25 DEC 83)

'84

20. The process has always been one of transformation
21. Is there such an animal as <u>ABSTRACT REALISM</u>?
22. Take the conceptual and crossbreed it with pure spontiety.
23. All overness defined in terms of light i.e., the nature of its source being spiritual from within.
24. There is <u>no</u> difineable formula
25. SPACE AIN'T NOTHING BUT TASTE!
26. The structure is trichotomy not dichotomy (my earlier interruption was shortsighted of me!)
27. Inner man + outer space = SPIRIT

⎫
⎬ 30 Jan. 84'
⎭

28. Am I addressing myself to a New Geometry or simply taking the old and locating it in another space?
29. In what way is my perspective different from Renaissance perspective?
30. If I throw out masculinity, If I throw out Regionality, If I throw out ethnicity, what am I left with? What risk are involved with doing this?

⎫
⎬ 9 FEB '84
⎭

31. I do not want to orchestrate Art History!
32. A NEW SPACE, A NEW PLACE, A NEW RENAISSANCE 10 FEB 84

18, 31, 32, 19, 27, 3

33. The spirit is <u>not</u> conceptual knowledge. 14 FEB 84
34. Each painting is a surprise!
35. I am not German. I have not commited any crimes ~~of~~ against humanity. My soul is not tortured. 16 FEB 84
36. Each painting is found. 17 FEB 84
37. There is madness out there + somebody's got to do something about it! 27 Feb 84

38. I am an <u>ENERGY FIELD</u> PAINTER. 28 Feb '84

39. I am more interested in what the color leaves behind; its' tracks. 3 March

40. I AM LOOKING FOR SOMETHING TO BASE MY LIFE UPON, A BELIEF SYSTEM, A REASON FOR LIVING. 6 MARCH

41. It's time that I come out of the closet. No longer can I remain anonymous. 8 March

42. I use this energy field to produce <u>magic objects</u> + each one must be different from the other. 12 March 84

43. MAYBE EVERYTHING THAT ARTISTS SAY IS BALONEY! 18 MARCH 84 (but such beautiful baloney!)

44. I am a carver of Light. 19 March

45. Sometimes I feel as if I am trying to steal western civilization. 22 March 84

46. <u>FREE THE SPIRIT!</u>

47. The plane is a substitute for the mask. 27 March '84

48. The "presence" that I speak of is something spiritual and it exist in space. 27 March 84

49. Maybe that Joseph Campbell is correct, society is always in need of Myth. Could my works fulfill that gap? 29 March

STUDIO LOG '98

4 OCT: I WANT TO REMOVE ME FROM THE PAINTING.

6 OCT: THE KEY TO REAL POWER LIE IN AESTHETICS. IF ONE CAN ESTABLISH AN ESTHETIC WHICH DEFINE TIME AS PRESENT IN THE MODERN TECHNOLOGICAL SOCIETY, THE POWER IS THEIRS.

8 OCT:

OBJECTIVES

1. REMOVE THE EUROPEAN SIGNIFANCE OF TOUCH IN PAINTING.
2. INSIST UPON THE PAINTING'S AFRICAN HERITAGE.
3. REMOVE THE NOTION OF ME.
4. STOP RELYING UPON GHOST TO DO THE PAINTING.
5. DON'T WALLOW IN THE PAST AND WITH GOD'S HELP AVOID ROMANTIC NATIONALISM.
6. THE PAINTING IS NOT AN ILLUSTRATION OF ANYTHING.
7. ELIMINATE THAT WHICH QUALIFIES AS NARRATIVE.
8. ALLOW THE PAINT AS MATERIAL TO TAKE CARE OF THE BLACK THING.
9. DON'T SUCCUMB TO POPULIST ESTHETICS.
10. LEARN TO UNDERSTAND EXISTENCE AS BEING POLITICAL.
11. EXCEPT THE FACT THAT THERE ARE MULTIPLE DIMENSIONS IN TIME.
12. DON'T EVER BEG FOR ANYTHING.
13. EXCEPT GOD'S GUIDANCE. AND FOREVER BE FREE.
14. LEARN TO LIVE BY THE PHILOSOPHY OF JAZZ.
15. ONLY FOOLS WANT TO BE FAMOUS (AVOID AT ALL COST)
16. THE PAINTING SHOULD NEVER EXIST AS A SQUARE, RECTANGLE, TRIANGLE OR ANY OTHER EUCLIDEAN FIGURE.
17. ABSTRACT EXPRESSIONIST GESTURE IS A NO-NO.
18. THE FIGURE IN PRESENT DAY PAINTING IS OBSOLETE UNTIL I REINTRODUCE IT AS A MODERN CONCEPT.
19. THE EUCLIDEAN GRID IN PAINTING IS OBSOLETE. IT MUST BE REPLACED BY THE FRACTAL GRID.
20. STAY AWAY FROM FALSE PRIMITIVE PATTERNS.
21. AVOID ART-WORLD STRAGETIES.
22. INSIST UPON PAINT ON CANVAS.
23. ERASE ALL KNOWN ISMS.
24. REVERSE THE ABSTRACT EXPRESSIONIST'S NOTION OF SPEED, SLOW IT DOWN.
25. BALANCE THE APPOLOIAN AND THE DIONYSION AT 50/50.
26. I MUST CHANGE THE COURSE OF ART HISTORY.
27. DON'T EVER USE THE PARASE AVANT GARDE.
28. LEARN TO HATE THE HISTORY OF ART AND ABOVE ALL DON'T TRUST IT.
29. THE PAINTING AS OBJECT MUST EXIST ON IT'S OWN TERMS.
30. USE SCIENCE AS METAPHOR.
31. BE THANKFUL AND PAY HOMAGE TO HORACE PIPPIN.
32. REMAIN TRUE TO MY SELF.

A list of "Objectives" from Whitten's studio notes, October 4–8, 1998

STUDIO LOG '98

4 OCT: I WANT TO REMOVE <u>ME</u> FROM THE PAINTING.

6 OCT: THE KEY TO REAL POWER LIE IN AESTHETICS. If ONE CAN ESTABLISH AN ESTHETIC WHICH DEFINE TIME AS PRESENT IN THE MODERN TECHNOLOGICAL SOCIETY, THE POWER IS THEIRS.

8 OCT: <u>OBJECTIVES</u>
1. REMOVE THE EUROPEAN SIGNIFANCE OF TOUCH IN PAINTING.
2. INSIST UPON THE PAINTING'S AFRICAN HERITAGE.
3. REMOVE THE NOTION OF ME.
4. STOP RELYING UPON GHOST TO DO THE PAINTING.
5. DON'T WALLOW IN THE PAST AND WITH GOD'S HELP AVOID ROMANTIC NATIONALISM.
6. THE PAINTING IS NOT AN ILLUSTRATION OF ANYTHING.
7. ELIMINATE THAT WHICH QUALIFIES AS NARRATIVE.
8. ALLOW THE PAINT AS MATERIAL TO TAKE CARE OF THE BLACK THING.
9. DON'T SUCCUMB TO POPULIST ESTHETICS.
10. LEARN TO UNDERSTAND EXISTENCE AS BEING POLITICAL.
11. EXCEPT THE FACT THAT THERE ARE MULTIPLE DIMENSIONS IN TIME.
12. DON'T EVER BEG FOR ANYTHING.
13. EXCEPT GOD'S GUIDANCE. AND FOREVER BE FREE.
14. LEARN TO LIVE BY THE PHILOSOPHY OF JAZZ.
15. ONLY FOOLS WANT TO BE FAMOUS (AVOID AT ALL COST)

16. THE PAINTING SHOULD NEVER EXIST AS A SQUARE, RECTANGLE, TRIANGEL OR ANY OTHER EUCLIDEAN FIGURE.
17. ABSTRACT EXPRESSIONIST GESTURE IS A NO-NO.
18. THE FIGURE IN PRESENT DAY PAINTING IS OBSOLETE UNTIL I REINTRODUCE IT AS A MODERN CONCEPT.
19. THE EUCLIDEAN GRID IN PAINTING IS OBSOLETE. IT MUST BE REPLACED BY THE FRACTAL GRID.
20. STAY AWAY FROM FALSE PRIMITIVE PATTERNS.
21. AVOID ART-WORLD STRAGETIES.
22. INSIST UPON PAINT ON CANVAS.
23. ERASE ALL KNOWN ISMS.
24. REVERSE THE ABSTRACT EXPRESSIONIST'S NOTION OF SPEED, SLOW IT DOWN.
25. BALANCE THE APPOLOIAN AND THE DIONYSION AT 50/50.
26. I MUST CHANGE THE COURSE OF ART HISTORY.
27. DON'T EVER USE THE PHRASE AVANT GARDE.
28. LEARN TO HATE THE HISTORY OF ART AND ABOVE ALL DON'T TRUST IT.
29. THE PAINTING AS OBJECT MUST EXIST ON ITS OWN TERMS.
30. USE SCIENCE AS METAPHOR.
31. BE THANKFUL AND PAY HOMAGE TO HORACE PIPPIN.
32. REMAIN TRUE TO MY SELF.

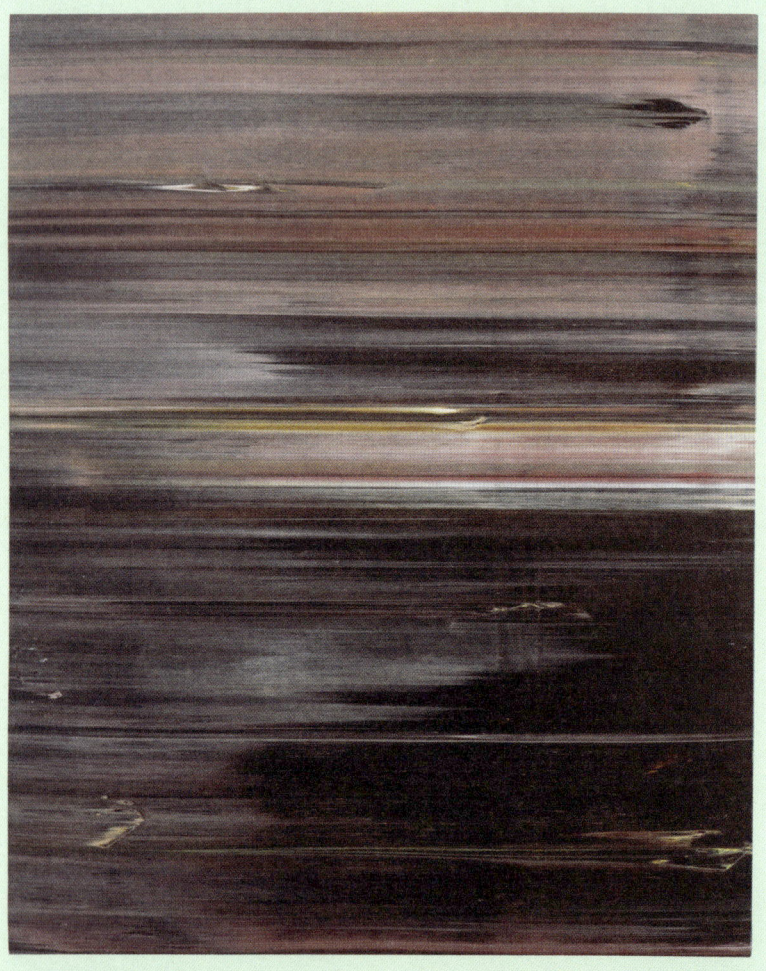

Black Table Setting (Homage to Duke Ellington), 1974. Acrylic on canvas, 72 × 60 in. (182.9 × 152.4 cm)

"I Am the Son of Jazz"

Whitten's *Black Table Setting (Homage to Duke Ellington)* (1974) features what seems like a fine series of waves with colors blending into colors, as when a moving body of water reflects a sunset. When the great jazz pianist died on May 24, 1974, Whitten noted, "THE DUKE WENT OUT TODAY... It's not often that we have such giants of men to shape our esthetics." A quick look through Whitten's oeuvre reveals his reverence for jazz was an essential part of what guided his choices in his practice as an artist. How did he come to take jazz so seriously?

While growing up in Bessemer, Alabama, Whitten played tenor saxophone for the Dunbar High School marching band and was introduced to the music of the classical jazz masters—John Coltrane, Miles Davis, Dizzy Gillespie, Thelonious Monk, Charlie Parker—by the band instructor. He enjoyed this music so much that he and his friends in the band formed their own jazz group, the Dunbar Jazzettes. They made some money playing dances and doing local radio commercials, and he soon began to fancy himself a possible professional. But when Whitten moved to New York and visited all the jazz hotspots—Birdland, the Blue Coronet, the Five Spot Cafe, Minton's, the Village Vanguard, the Half Note—and heard, for the first time, accomplished jazz musicians play live, he understood that he was not cut out to be one of them. Nonetheless, he also recognized that his relationship with jazz was not that of a mere enthusiast.

In jazz, Whitten found sensibilities and approaches he believed any artist seeking the highest quality in their work should strive to embrace and emulate. He also

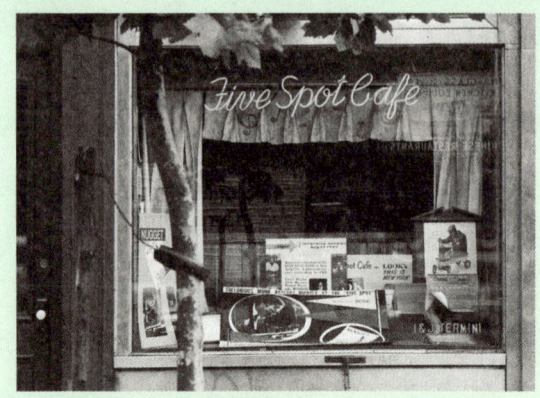

The Five Spot Cafe at 5 Cooper Square, New York, ca. 1957

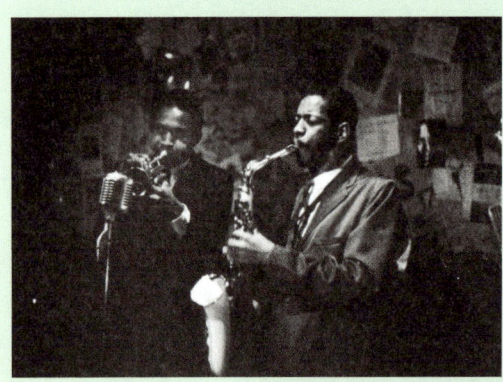

Ornette Coleman and Don Cherry performing at the Five Spot Cafe, New York, 1959

John Coltrane performing at the Half Note Club, New York, 1965

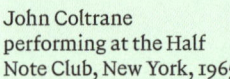

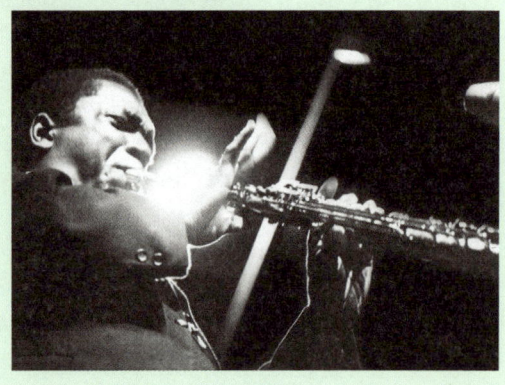

Influences

found a kinship with jazz musicians because of his own dissatisfaction with existing forms and aesthetics—in his case, Abstract Expressionism. Jazz, too, demanded endless experimentation and innovation; its practitioners were using instruments designed to produce European and classical music to instead create new and unbelievable sounds. The music also had its own kind of science, which intersected with Whitten's own interest in technological advancements and modern inventions.

At the Blue Coronet Club in Brooklyn, Whitten met Coltrane, who explained that he thought of music as coming to him in sheets of sound, and that he would only catch as many sheets as he needed. This formed the basis of Whitten's analogous concept of "planar light": the way light passed through his paintings in sheets, too, with multicolored tesserae absorbing and reflecting light differently. Whitten was alert to how large edifices—whether jazz compositions, paintings, or whole universes—are made of tiny components. Indeed, toward the end of his life, on March 31, 2017, he wrote in his notes, "Molecular perception is the key. With this key I can open all doors (portals) into another universe. The other universe is my way of expanding consciousness.... When consciousness expands freedom expands. Remember jazz is the expansion of freedom and I am the son of jazz."

Jazz also influenced the way Whitten understood the notion of artistic style. In 1994, as a guest on Charlie Finch's radio program "Art Breaking" on WBAI, Whitten explained, "Style is a bad word for me.... I say beware of style. I'm not hindered by style at all. Style is a look, an appearance, and I always make an emphasis upon saying what's more important is what drives the thing, not so much what it looks like, or the repetition of what it looks like. So as a result, my works have a broad look about them." Connecting this back to jazz, he explained that this understanding could be applied to Coltrane's music, too, for example: "You hear John Coltrane, [and] there is a... certain glue to John Coltrane that repeats itself, but in terms of how it comes out, it can be very different."

Homecoming: For Miles (1992) gives a good sense of Whitten's feelings about jazz, painting, and technology, depicting what looks simultaneously like a galaxy and a computer screen. A giant circle and lines, all dotted like a geometric diagram, announce a mathematical presence, as though the galaxy itself were trying to work out its own constellation. This is how Whitten perceived Davis's music, and jazz in general: soul-searching, large, triumphant.

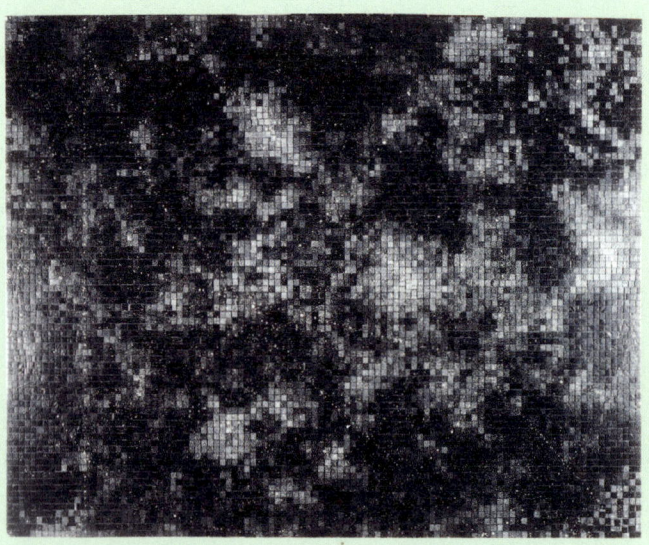

Homecoming: For Miles, 1992. Acrylic on canvas, 81¼ × 105½ in. (206.4 × 268 cm)

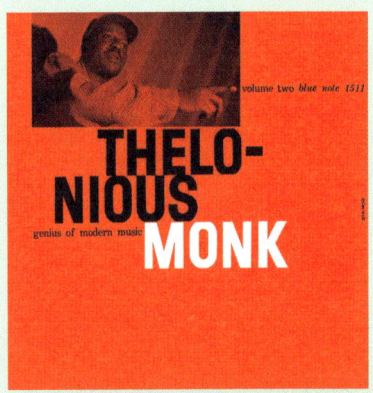
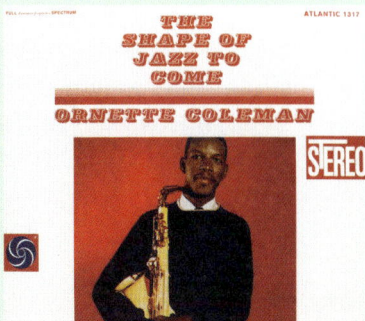
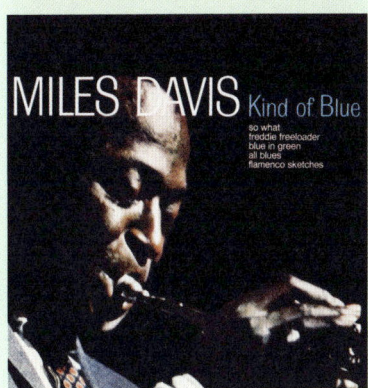
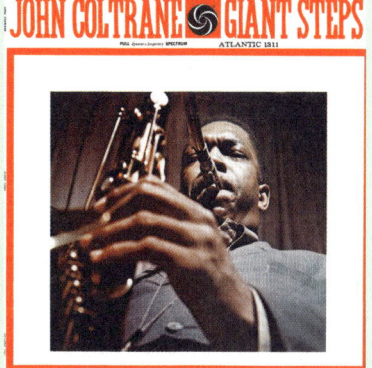

Four of Whitten's favorites from his jazz collection:
Thelonious Monk's *Genius of Modern Music Vol. 2*
(1952), Ornette Coleman's *The Shape of Jazz to
Come* (1959), Miles Davis's *Kind of Blue* (1959),
and John Coltrane's *Giant Steps* (1960)

"Five Lines Four Spaces"

In 2012, Whitten was included in *Blues for Smoke*
at the Museum of Contemporary Art, Los Angeles,
curated by Bennett Simpson. The exhibition
explored art and other media through the blues.
Simpson invited Whitten to write an essay,
reproduced here, for the catalogue. Whitten
noted that it was "a great opportunity to get
my ideas about jazz in print. I have a lot to say!"

Now is the time. When my white slave masters discovered
that my drum was a subversive instrument they took it from
me. My time was stolen. To steal a man's time is an attempt
to steal his soul. The only instrument available was my body,
so I used my skin: I clapped my hands, slapped my thighs,
and stomped my feet in dynamic rhythms. I stretched my
mouth wide open and allowed my vocal chords to strike
a primal cry. I forced the world to listen. I discovered that
my pain was a universal pain. Even those who could not
understand my native language could understand my pain.

Born in the slave fields of the Deep South, call and refrain
is the cornerstone of jazz and blues. Dialogue, however
painful, starts between two or more people.... I call,
you answer. How I feel is always about power: I, and only I,
have control of my feelings. Empowerment serves identity
and identity is an act of will. Beyond the political there is
always the power of love. Whether in the guise of the divine
or celebrated in the joy of sex, jazz and blues continue
to inspire the power of love.

Time is a memory bank. The past, present, and future
are encoded in time. Art can be used as a tool to decipher

time. Break the code and consciousness will expand. When consciousness expands, freedom expands. The philosophical underpinning of jazz is the expansion of freedom. We have entered third-stage modernism, which is a global aesthetic based on otherness. Like jazz, third-stage modernism insists on the expansion of freedom. Experimentation is the key. I believe that there are sounds we have not heard. I believe that there are colors we have not seen. And I believe that there are feelings yet to be felt.

Postmodernism was a welcome intermission. It allowed an opening for all the various multicultural, disinherited, and fragmented sensibilities to make their voices heard. First- and second-stage modernism did not acknowledge any artistic contribution by African Americans; such inclusion was simply not an issue worthy of consideration. Third-stage modernism, with its emphasis on otherness and inclusion, offers the best scenario of hope for reconciliation. Without hope there is no reason for freedom. Anarchy is not a viable option, and romantic nihilism is only an immature, masturbatory response to the threat of total planetary chaos. We must learn to overcome our existentialist notion of being.

Abstract artists are attracted to jazz because of its expandable qualities. Jazz imposes no limit on feeling and its basic elements of spontaneity/improvisation preserve freshness of spirit. Spirit does not like stale air! Spontaneity/improvisation are necessary ingredients of art. The acceptance of spontaneity/improvisation does not reject the value of conceptual thought. Conceptualism is a tool in the service of spontaneity/improvisation. The multidimensional sheets of sound in John Coltrane's music could not reach cognition without the conceptual. As an abstract painter, I translate Coltrane's sheets of sound into sheets of light.

Every emotion that ripples through my body is compressed into a plane of light.

My light is a physical fact: I freeze, boil, burn, hammer, saw, sand, grind, and glue sheets of acrylic paint with weights and clamps. The paint is the light. Being a physical fact, it is therefore concrete. The concrete must be transcended through sensibility in order to become abstract. For me, abstraction is a matter of choice, and transcendence is not attributed to any divine ordinance. I spoke of empowerment serving identity; likewise, transcendence empowers us to overcome. "We Shall Overcome" was not on arbitrary gesture of defiance. It was, and is, an act of identity.

Now is the time. Every day in the studio is an adventure. Formal materialism is only a means; it is not an end. Matter is dead meat without spirit. Spirit lives in sensibility. Sensibility, and only sensibility, makes art possible. Plasticity makes sensibility visual. My cosmic guides are: John Coltrane, Thelonious Monk, Charlie Parker, Miles Davis, Charles Mingus, Kenny Dorham, Bud Powell, Ron Carter, Fats Navarro, Dexter Gordon, Cecil Taylor, Ornette Coleman, Sonny Rollins, Coleman Hawkins, Eric Dolphy, Albert Ayler, Sun Ra, Clifford Brown... I am so blessed.

The historical continuity of jazz and blues is a valuable cultural asset. For the artist, especially the abstract artist, it is raw material, a resource of infinite possibilities available to anyone capable of deciphering its emotional codes. Good news, I found my stolen drum. I found it while experimenting with the formal element of space. Evidently, Rashied Ali, Alvin Jones, Philly Jo Jones, Art Blakey, Max Roach, Roy Haynes, Arthur Taylor, and others had retrieved it and stashed it in deep space.

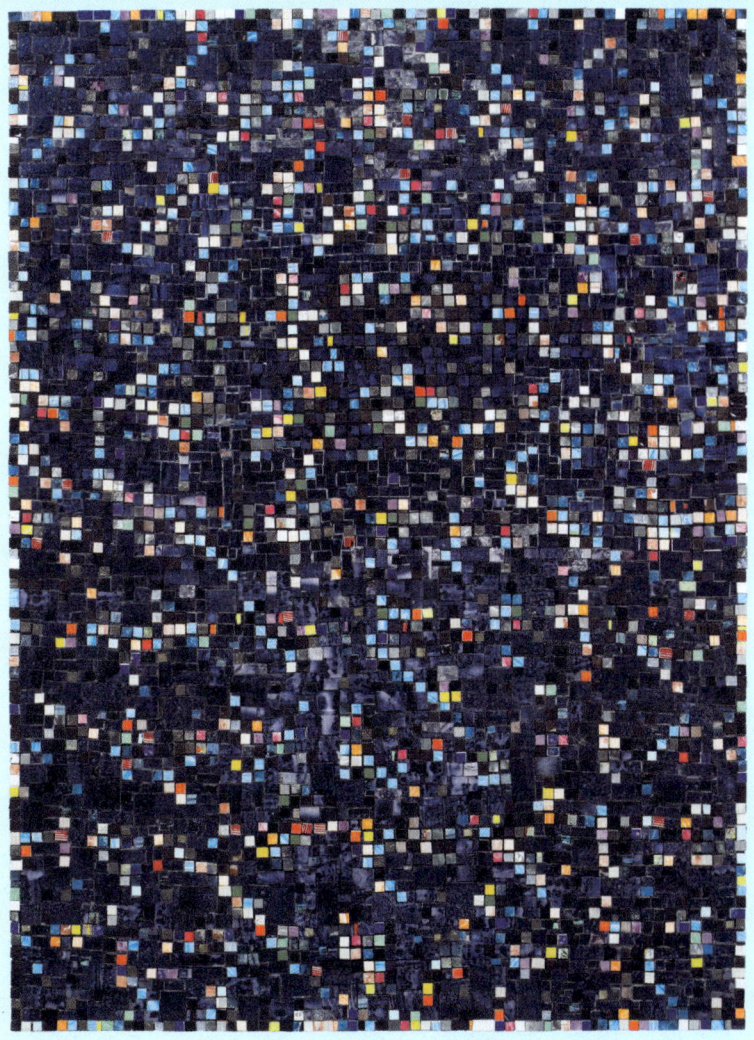

Five Lines Four Spaces (An Updated Version Of The Broadway Boogie Woogie): For Bud Powell, 2011. Acrylic on canvas, 62 × 46¾ in. (157.5 × 118.7 cm). Detail, pp. 126–27

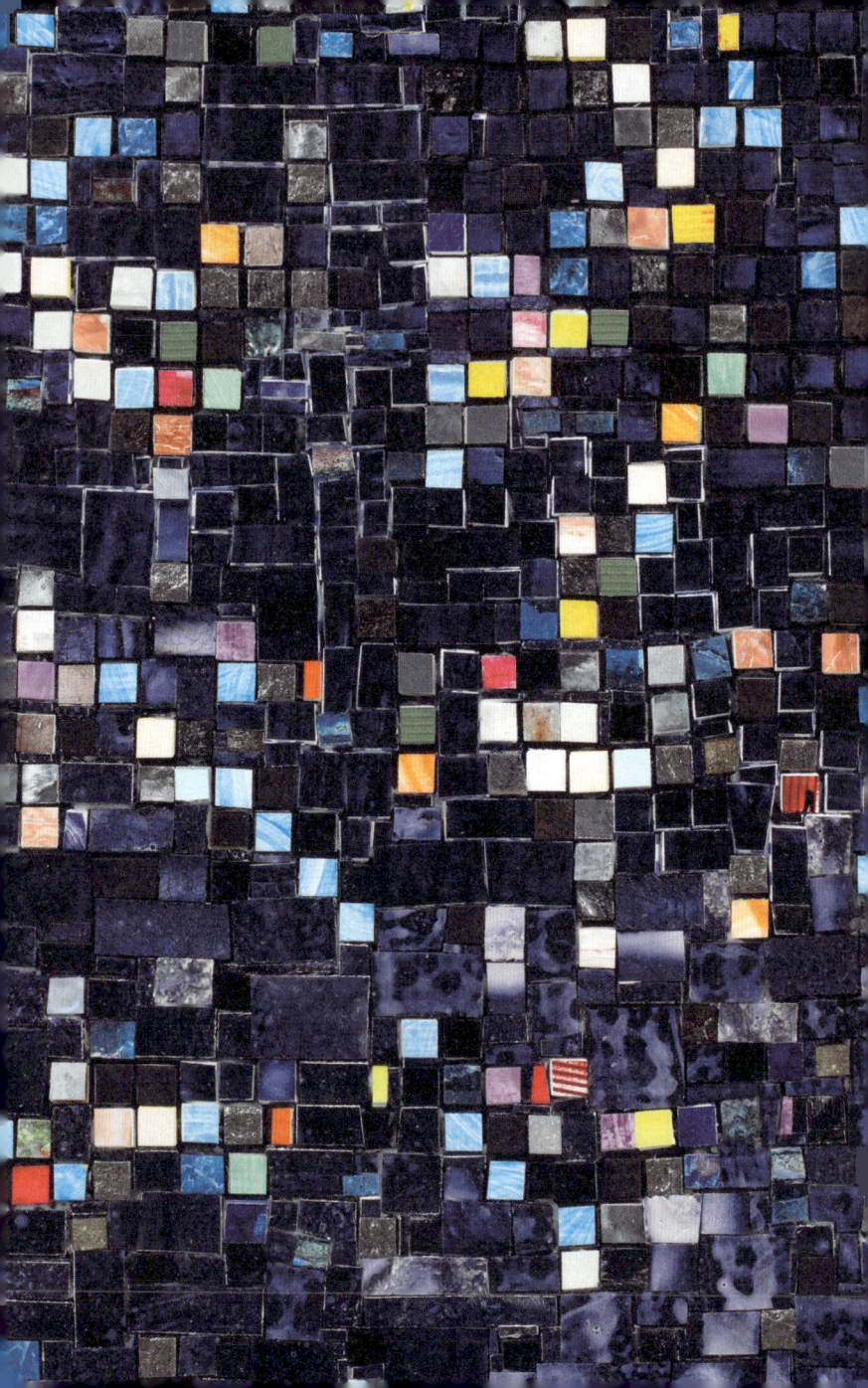

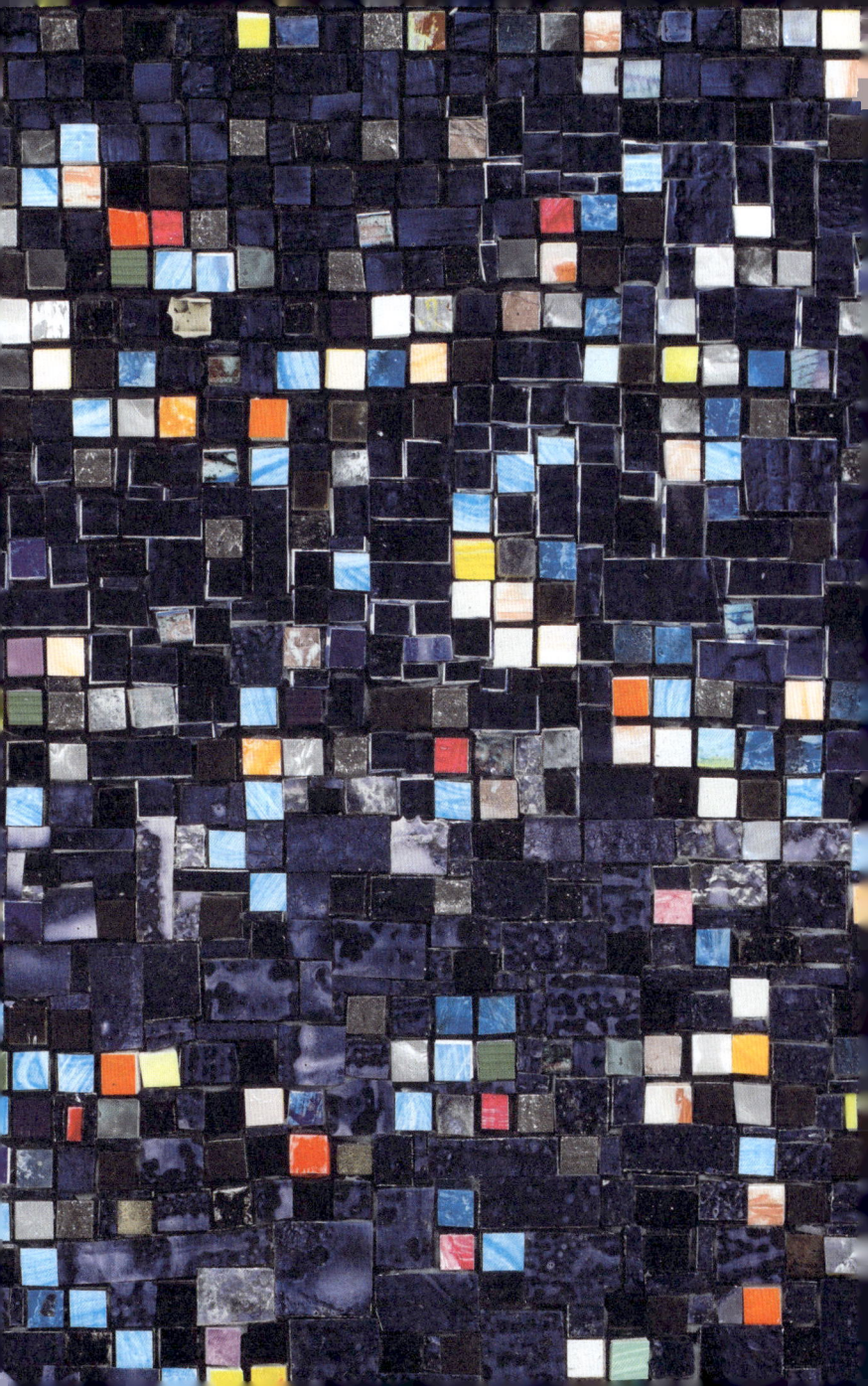

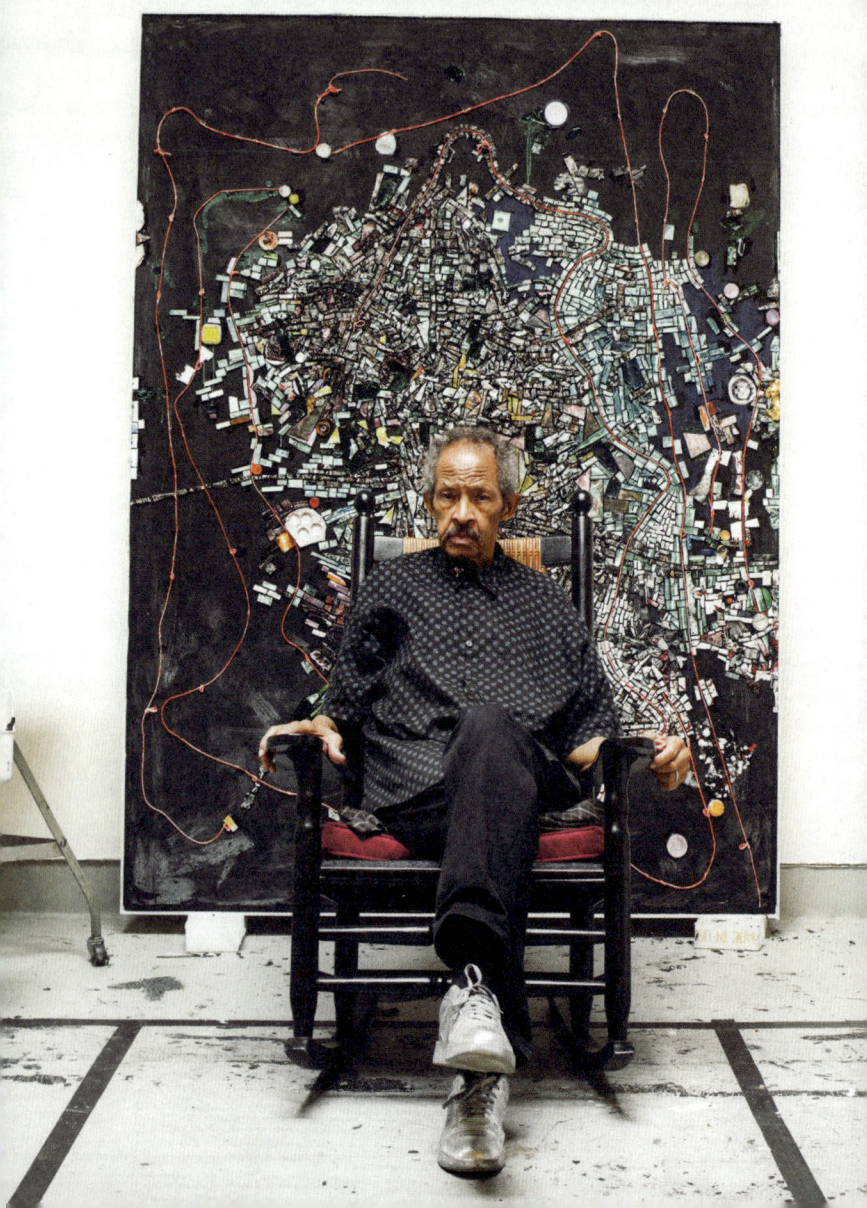

Whitten in his Woodside, Queens, studio with *Black Monolith XI, (Six Kinky Strings: For Chuck Berry)* in progress behind him, ca. 2017; the finished work is oriented differently, with what is the top here at the bottom

Black Monoliths

Whitten was committed to preserving memories: the memories of those he loved, those who influenced him, and those to whom he felt connected culturally. *Black Monoliths*, his most famous series taking this approach, memorializes Black icons from literature, music, politics, sports, and visual art. Whitten named the series, which he began in 1988 and continued until his death, after a giant stone behind his house in Crete.

The first painting in the series was *Black Monolith I, A Tribute to James Baldwin* (p. 132), dedicated to the eponymous writer whom Whitten had met many times and whose books he praised for "putting words into the feelings that I had had about how we react to this system we are born into." It is one of the more dense paintings Whitten ever made, with multiple coats of black acrylic scarified by aluminum sheets, bubble wrap, tire treads, paint cans, and striated rubber mats. In the center is a textured mass that forms the shape of a head in profile, all in black. Other colors seep in around the edges of the painting: a red smear on the top left; blues under a peeling green and white layer; small, unexpected yellows underneath what look like tire tracks. The painting itself is large—eight feet by six feet, ten inches—and is the only one in the series that Whitten didn't construct from his signature tesserae.

Whitten continued with *Black Monolith II, Homage To Ralph Ellison The Invisible Man* (1994; p. 133), also honoring a writer. The painting centers what looks like a silhouette of a man, with pale blue, white, and yellow tesserae surrounding him like a halo. Ellison's title character loved light bulbs so much that he had 1,369 of them in his secret

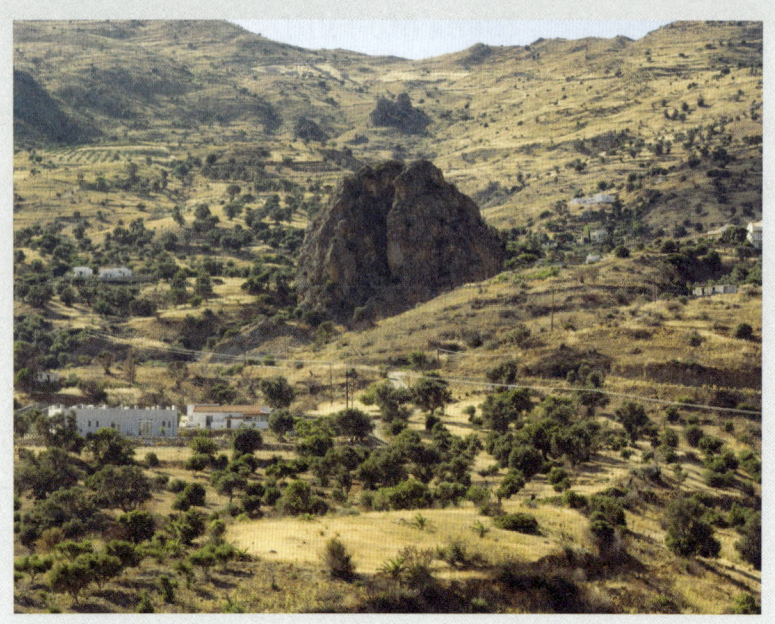

The Original Black Monolith

The title of the *Black Monoliths* series came from a massive stone monolith near Whitten's house in Crete, pictured here. "Just viewing it is so impressive," Whitten explained in his 2009 oral history for the Archives of American Art, Smithonian Institution. "That kind of a presence, all of those Black Monoliths had this massive presence about them." Indeed, reflecting in an unpublished note from 2016 on *Black Monolith X, (Birth of Muhammad Ali)*, he wrote, "I could spend the rest of my life adding to my series of Black Monolith paintings. There are so many Black Monoliths in the history of African-Americans. Our history of survival in America is defined both by the heroic deeds of the collective, and of the independent activists working in a variety of disciplines."

basement apartment. In Whitten's depiction, not only do the lights surround the figure but he himself seems to be afire, the orange tesserae at the core revealing an inner glow—in the face of invisibility, an assertion of identity in visual form. Similarly, *Black Monolith VIII, For Maya Angelou* (2015; p. 141), one of Whitten's later entries in the series, features a dark core with almost invisible tesserae flowing outward and becoming brighter as they approach the edge. The painting seems to acknowledge how the shared burdens of the time must have taken their toll on this venerated poet and activist—and yet how, even under such weight, she managed to continuously radiate light.

Whitten's memorials to his heroes continue to resonate because of the tenderness with which he considered each member in the series. These were people he learned from, people whose struggles he knew, people from a community that nourished him. It is appropriate, then, that today, it is in his work of memorializing others that Whitten is himself preserved.

Black Monolith I, A Tribute to James Baldwin, 1988. Acrylic on canvas, 96 × 82 in. (243.8 × 208.3 cm)

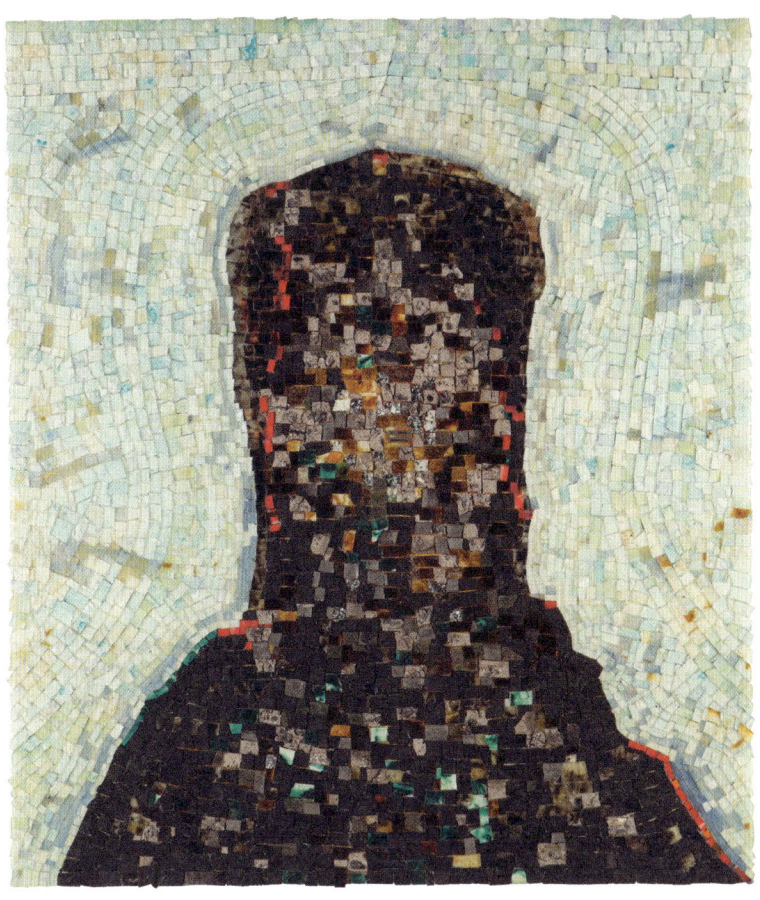

Black Monolith II, Homage To Ralph Ellison The Invisible Man, 1994. Acrylic, molasses, copper, salt, coal, ash, chocolate, onion, herbs, rust, eggshell, razor blade on canvas, 58½ × 52½ in. (148.6 × 133.4 cm). Detail, pp. 134–35

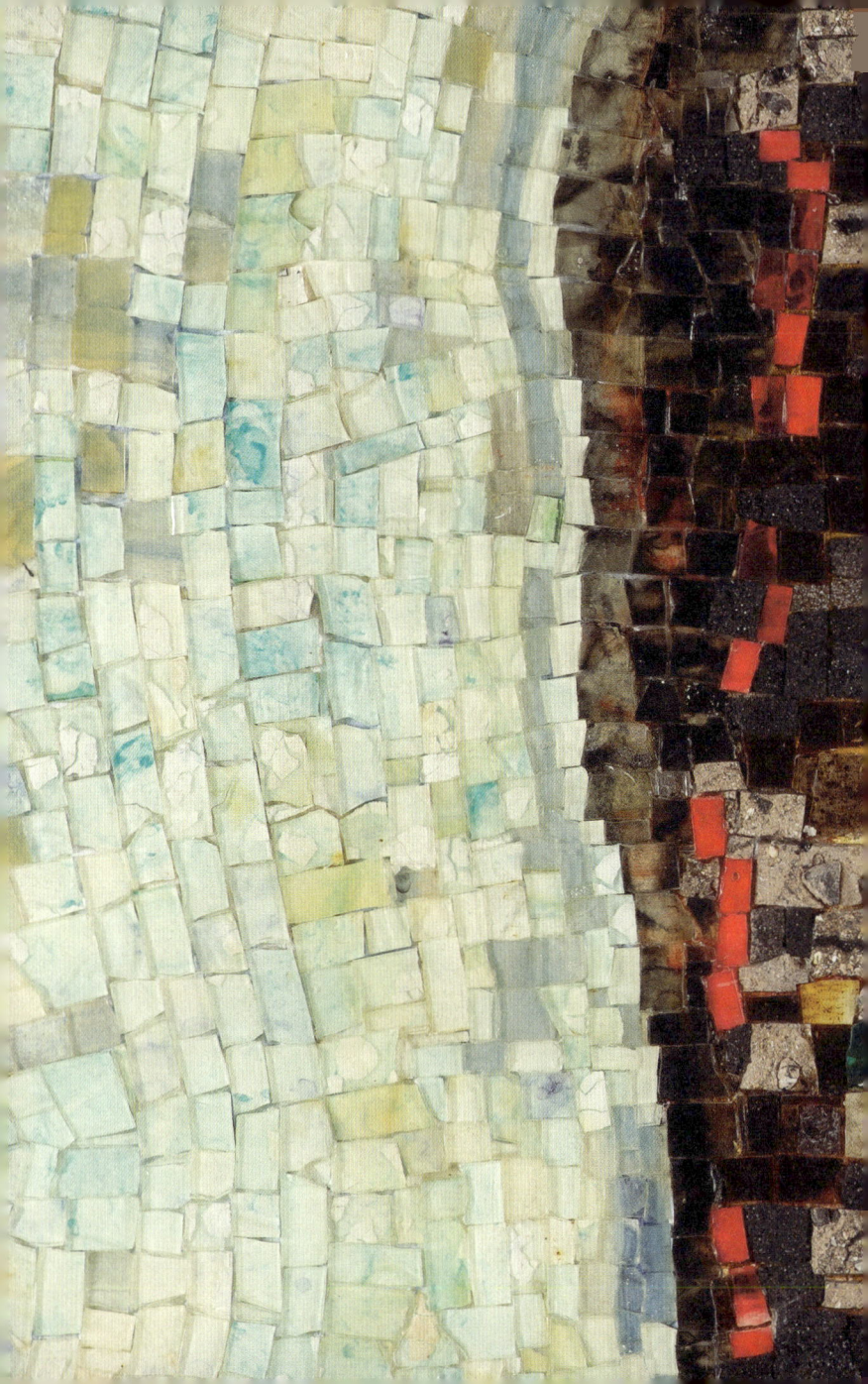

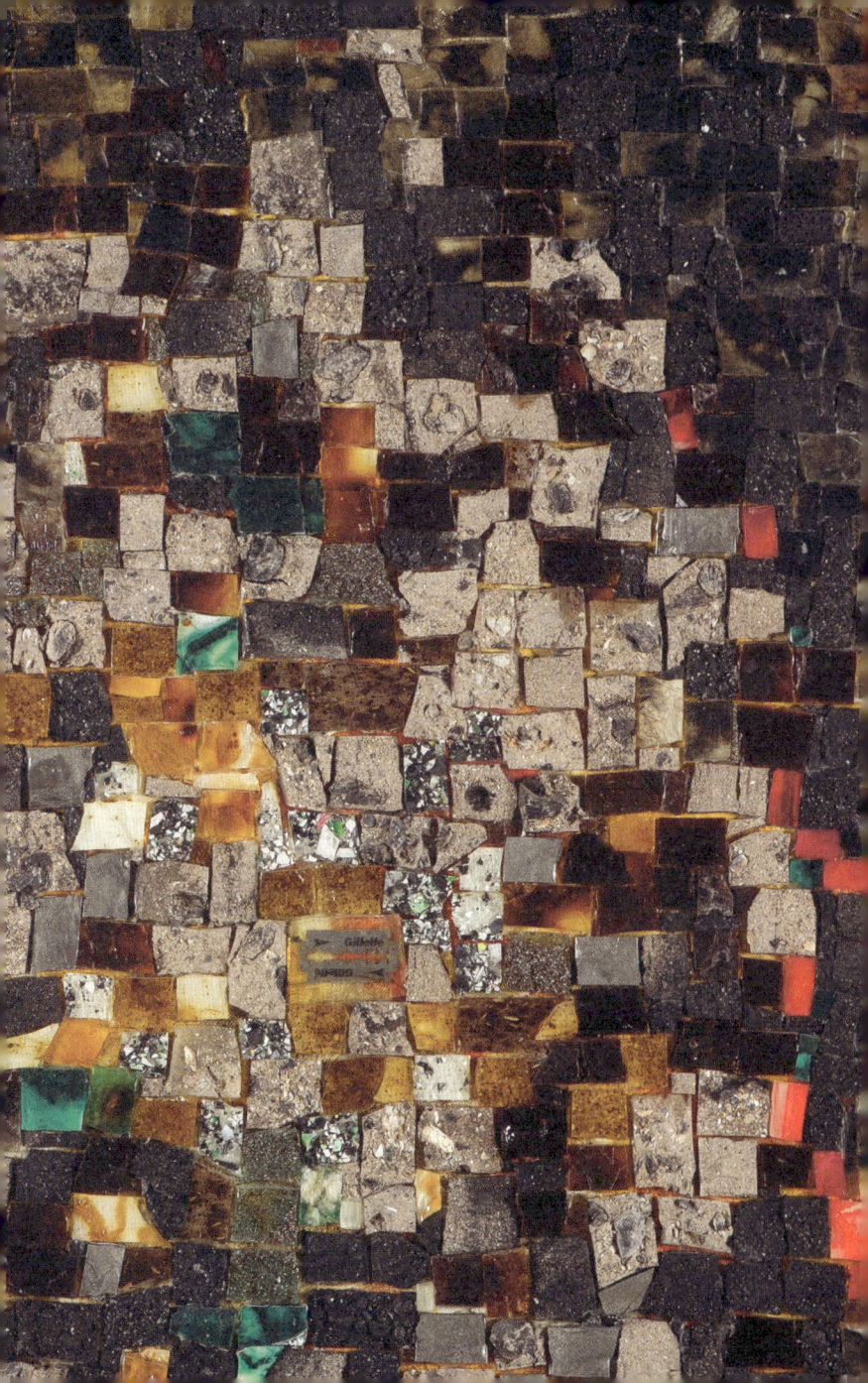

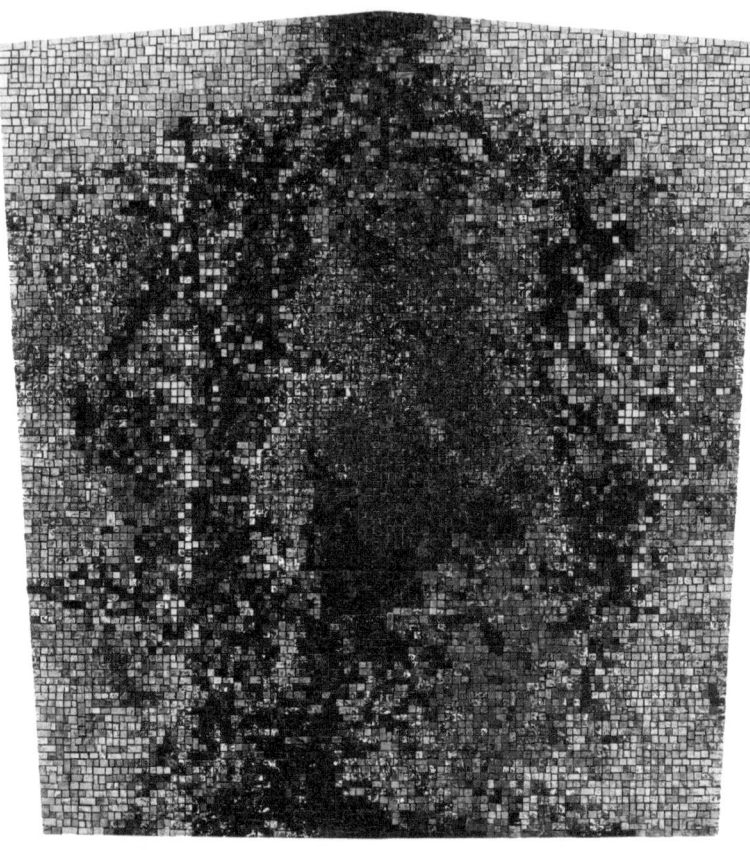

Black Monolith III, For Barbara Jordan, 1998. Acrylic collage on canvas, 69 × 65½ in. (175.3 × 166.4 cm)

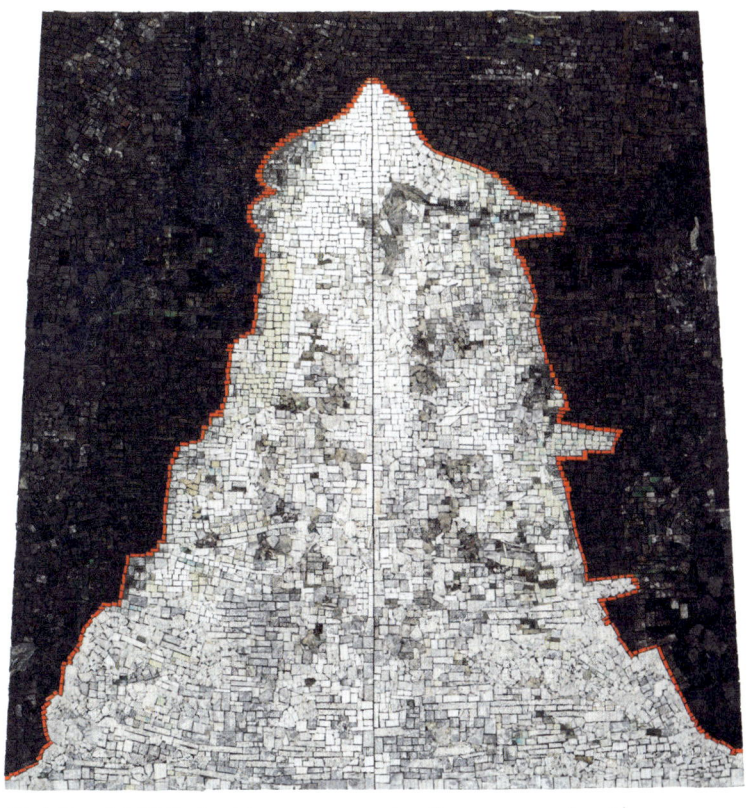

Black Monolith IV, For Jacob Lawrence, 2001. Acrylic on canvas, 96 × 96 in. (243.8 × 243.8 cm)

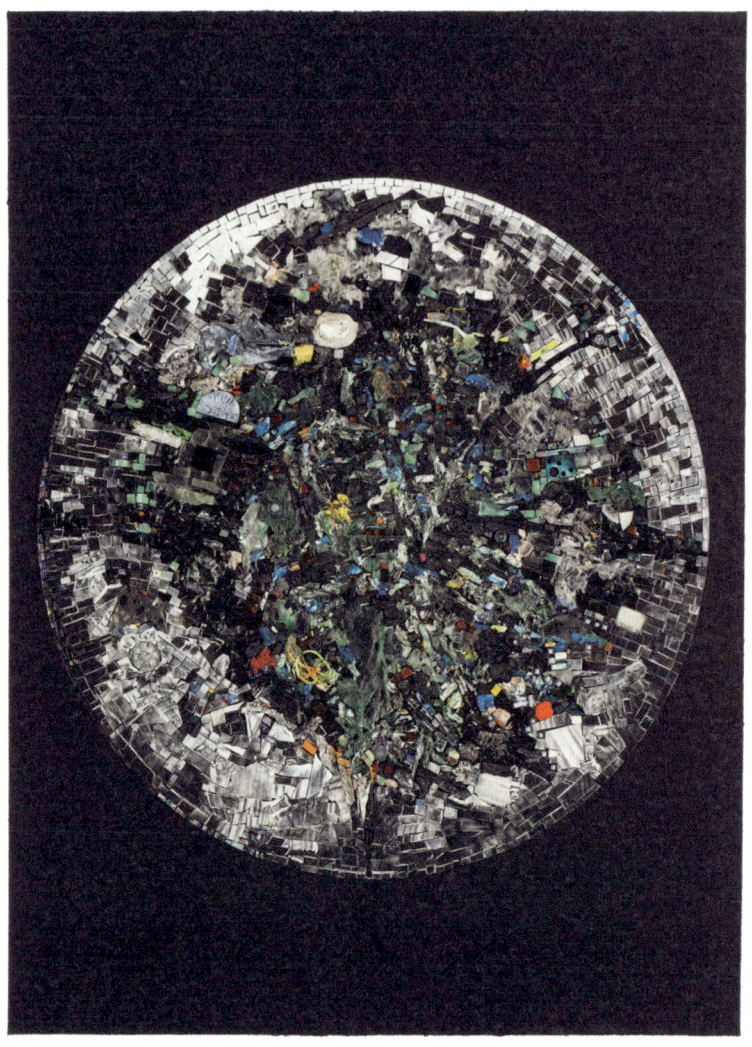

Black Monolith V, Full Circle: For LeRoi Jones A.K.A. Amiri Baraka, 2014. Acrylic on canvas 84 × 63 in. (213.4 × 160 cm)

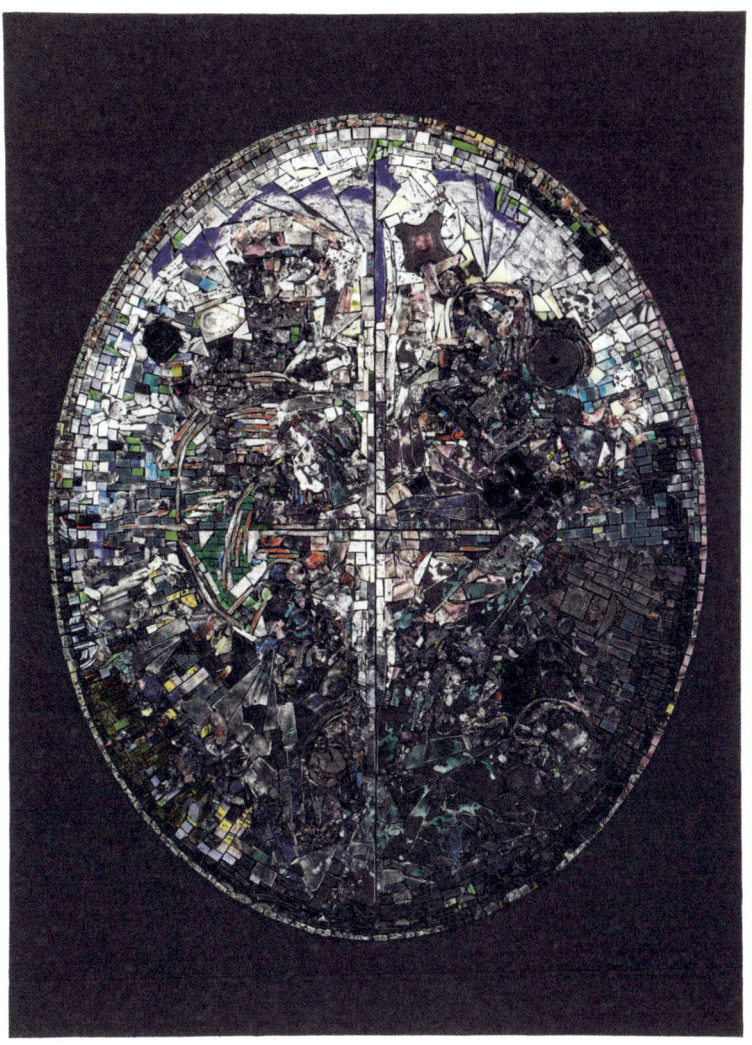

Black Monolith, VI Mask: (Updated Version) For Terry Adkins, 2014. Acrylic on canvas, 84¼ × 63¼ in. (214 × 160.7 cm)

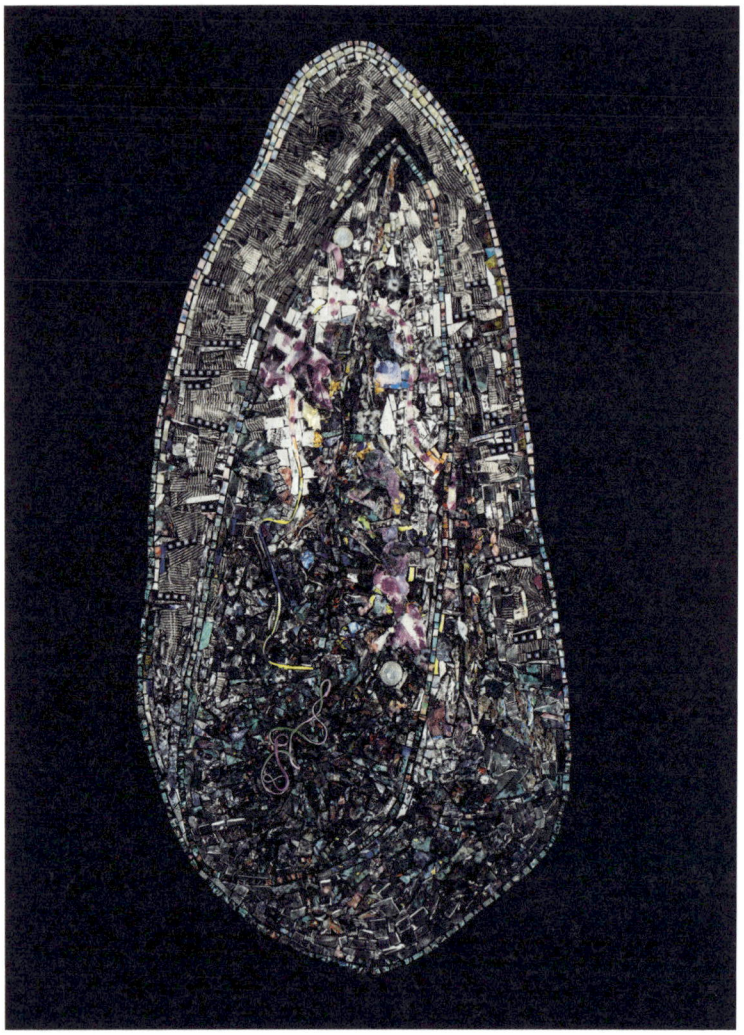

Black Monolith VII, Du Bois Legacy: For W. E. Burghardt, 2014. Acrylic on canvas, 84⅛ × 63⅛ in. (213.7 × 160.3 cm)

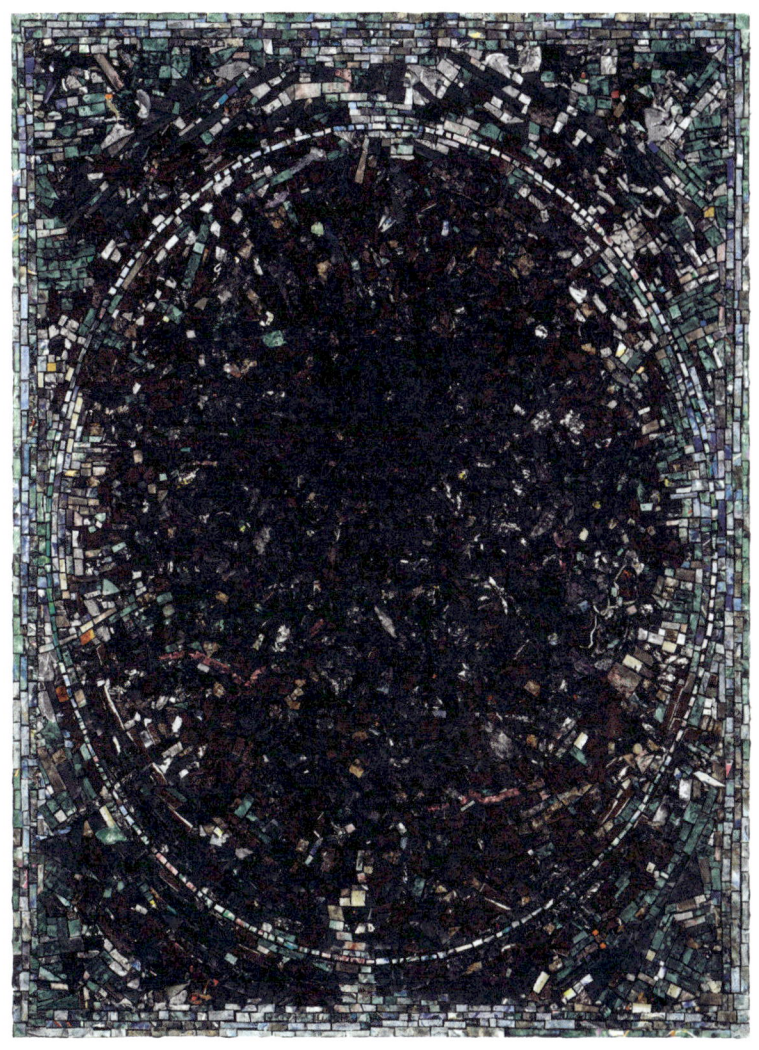

Black Monolith VIII, For Maya Angelou, 2015. Acrylic on canvas, 84 × 63 in. (213.4 × 160 cm)

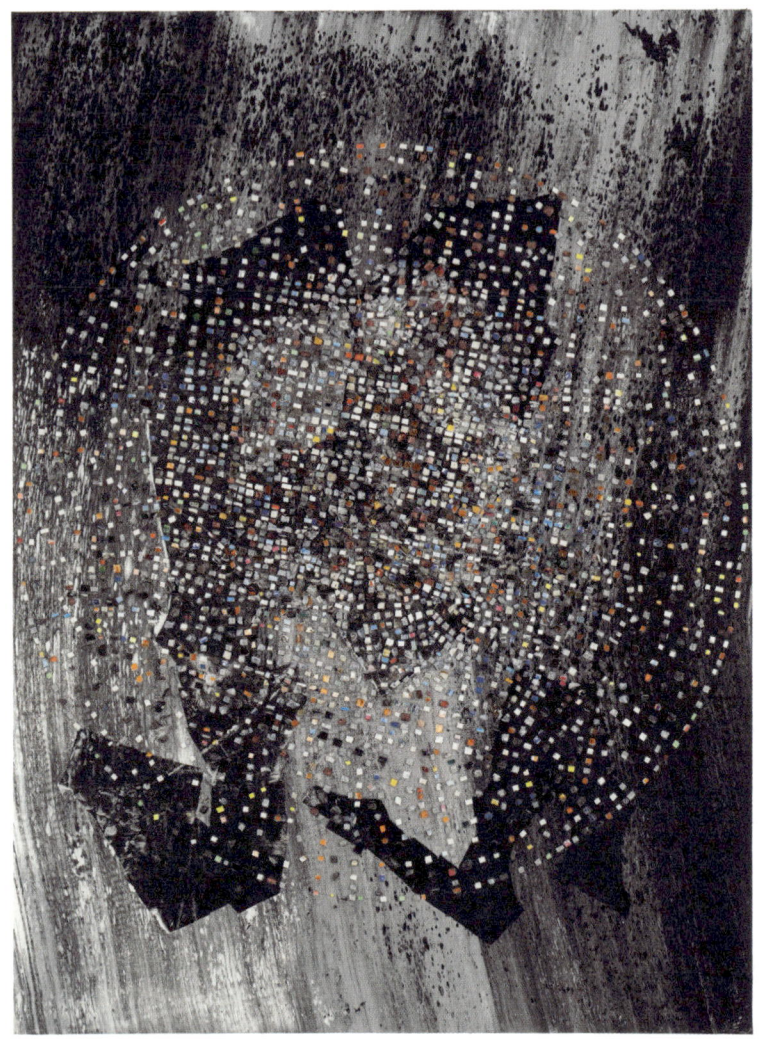

Black Monolith XI, (Open Circle For Ornette Coleman), 2015. Acrylic on canvas, 84 × 63 in. (213.4 × 160 cm)

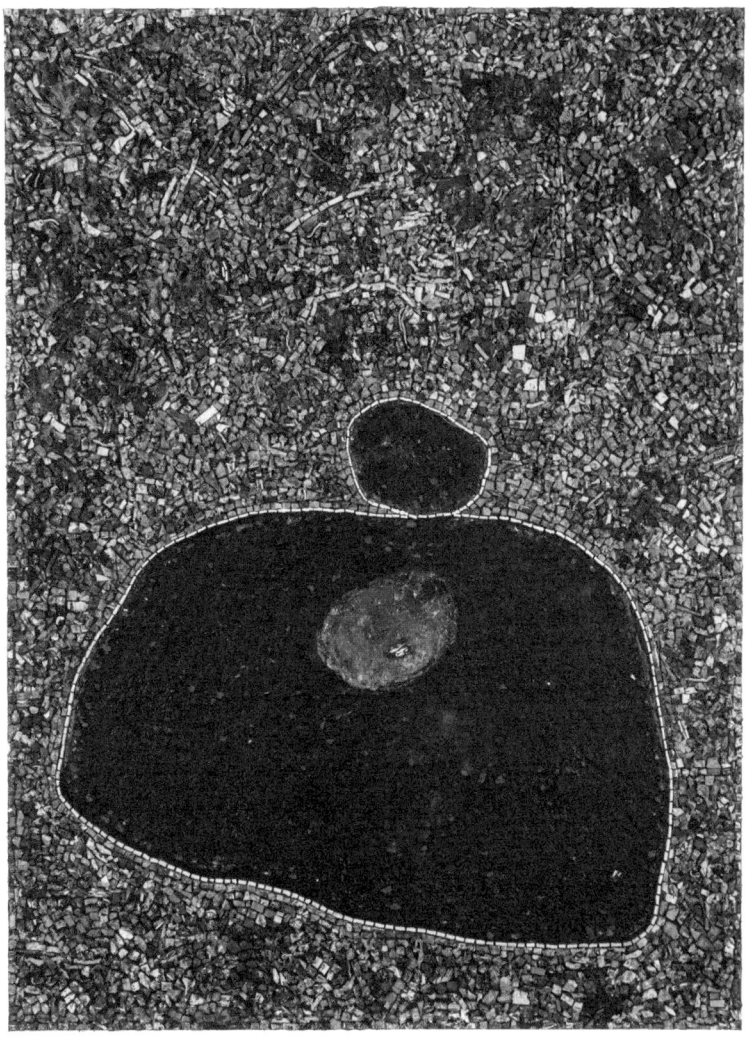

Black Monolith X, (Birth of Muhammad Ali), 2016. Acrylic on canvas, 84 × 63 in. (213.4 × 160 cm)

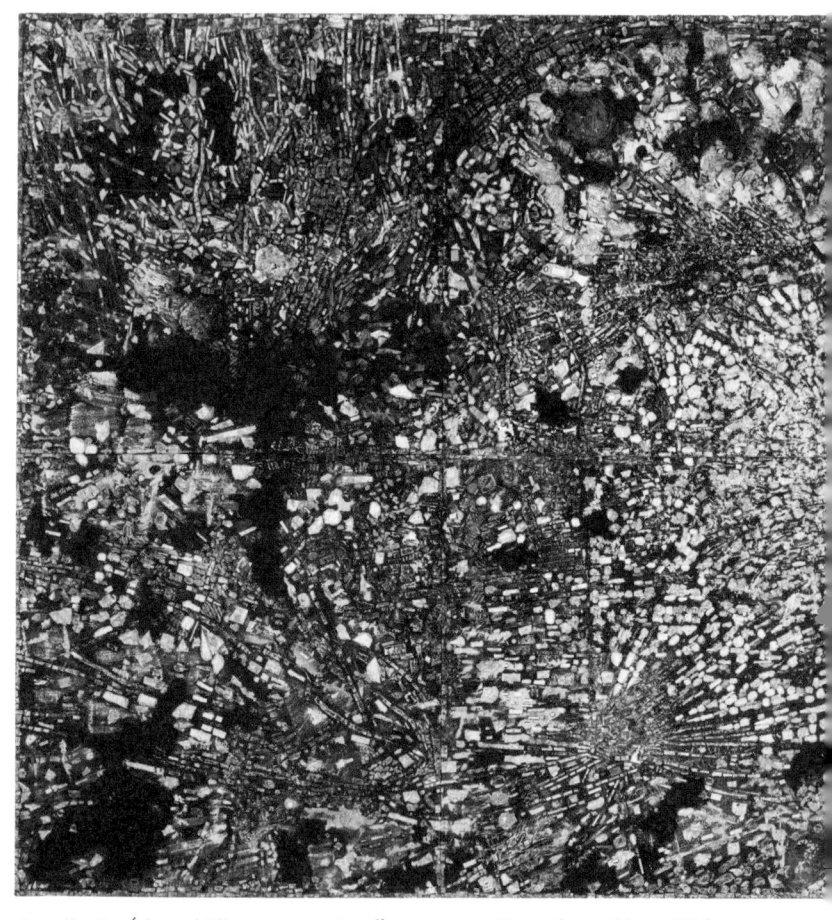

Atopolis: For Édouard Glissant, 2014. Acrylic on canvas, 8 panels, 124½ × 248½ in.
(316.2 × 631.2 cm)

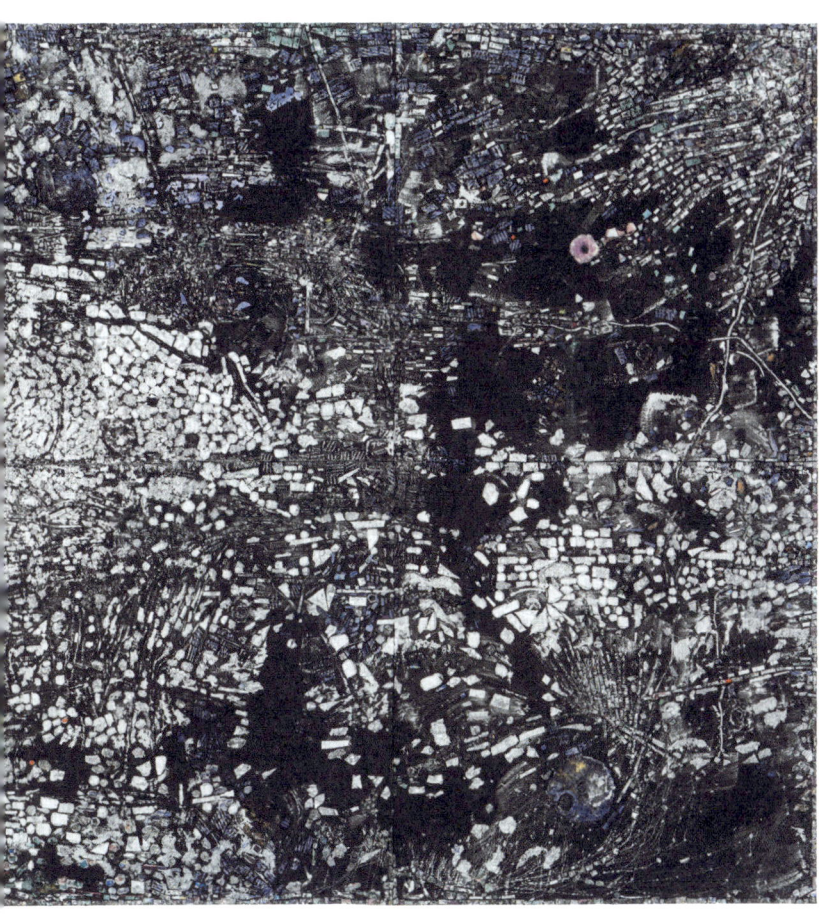

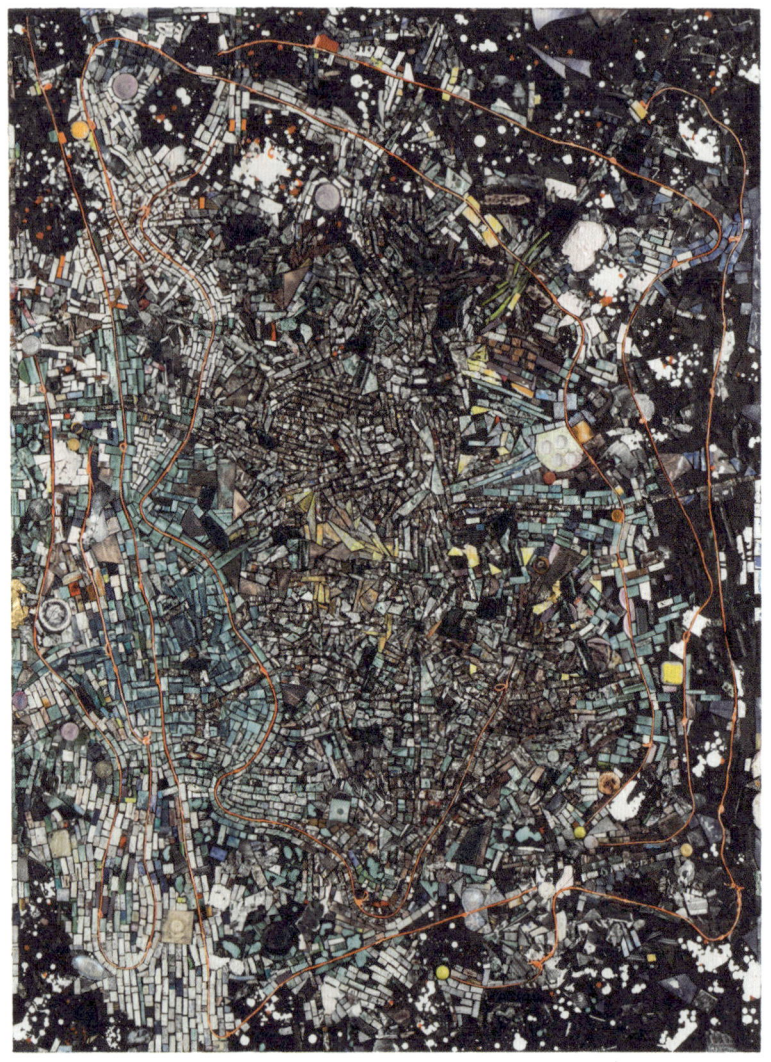

Black Monolith XI, (Six Kinky Strings: For Chuck Berry), 2017. Acrylic on canvas, 84 × 63 in. (213.4 × 160 cm). Detail opposite

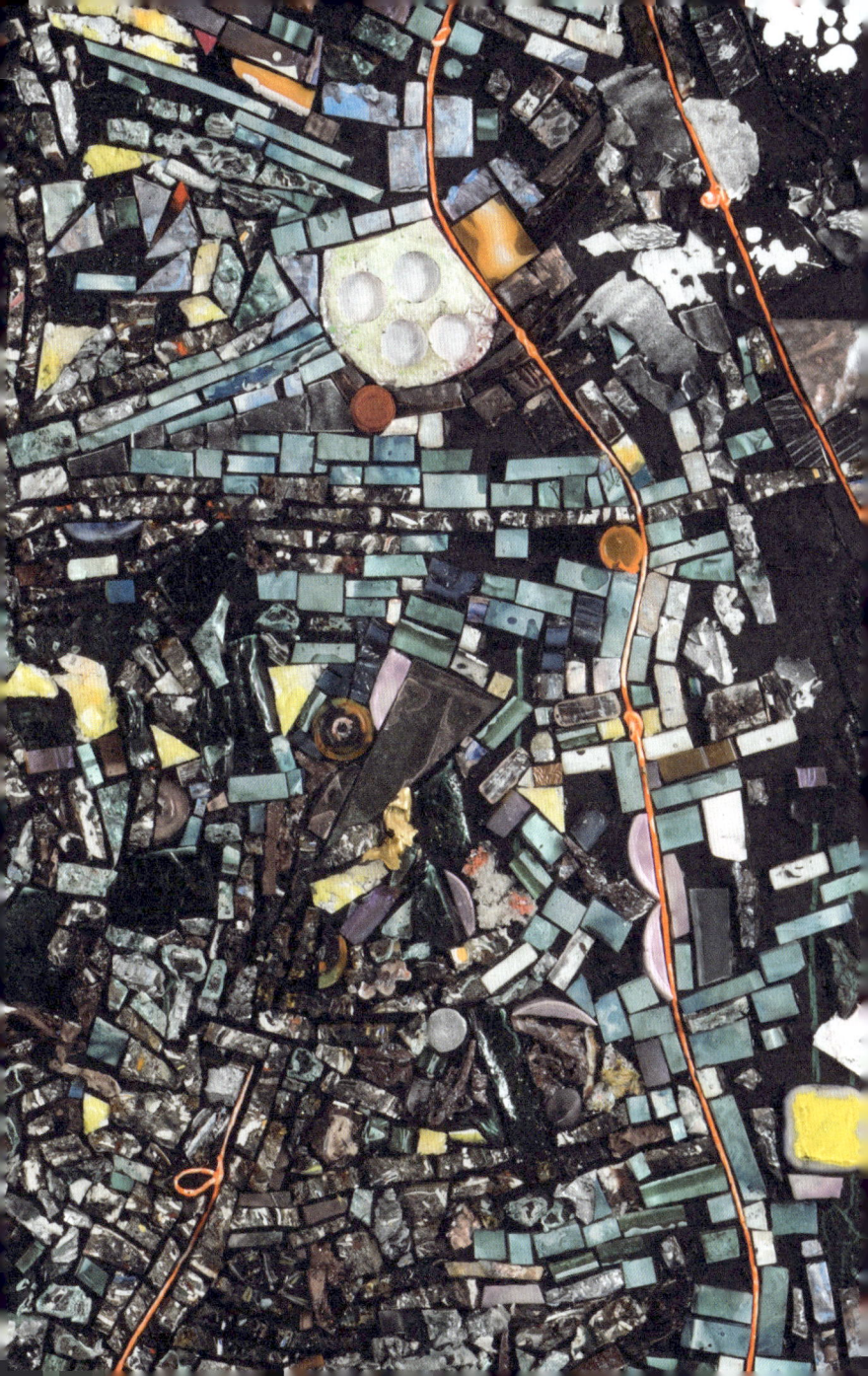

Chronology

1939 Born on December 5 in Bessemer, Alabama, to Annie B. and Mose Whitten, a seamstress and a coalminer.

1945–57 Attends segregated elementary, junior high, and high schools. Shows an early interest in art and music, playing tenor saxophone in the high school marching band and making posters and decorations for school dances.

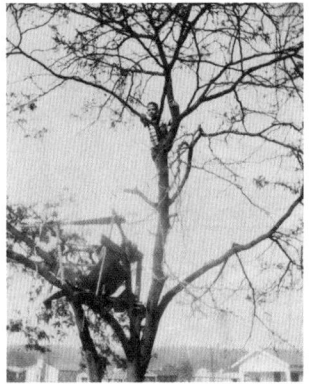

Whitten climbing a tree near his childhood home in Bessemer, Alabama, ca. 1949–50

1957 Enrolls in Tuskegee Institute (now Tuskegee University), a historically Black land-grant university in Tuskegee, Alabama, in the fall. An Air Force ROTC cadet, he majors in premedical studies and works part-time as a janitor as part of a work-study scholarship program.

Watches Martin Luther King Jr. speak at the Dexter Avenue Baptist Church in Montgomery, Alabama.

1958 In the summer, goes to New York for the first time, working as a sous-chef in the kitchen of a Jewish hotel in the Catskills to earn money for school.

1959 Transfers to Southern University in Baton Rouge, Louisiana, to study art. Returns to New York that summer and works at a construction site in Brooklyn.

1960 Co-organizes a civil rights march through downtown Baton Rouge in the spring semester. After the protest turns violent, decides to leave the South and move to New York. Arrives in time to take the entrance examination for Cooper Union and is accepted for the fall semester.

Lives in the back of his studio, a storefront at 369 East Tenth Street between Avenues B and C in Manhattan.

Begins to immerse himself in the city's art scene, frequenting bars such as Stanley's and Cedar Bar, an Abstract Expressionist hangout. Meets many influential artists, writers, and musicians, including Emilio Cruz, Philip Guston, Franz Kline, Willem de Kooning, Joe Overstreet, and Bob Thompson; Ishmael Reed; and Ornette Coleman, Miles Davis, Kenny Dorham, and Thelonious Monk.

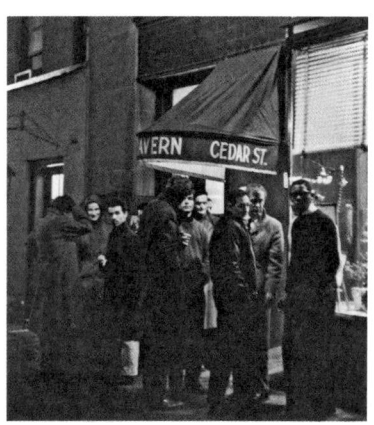

Patrons outside the Cedar Street Tavern at 24 University Place, New York, 1959

1962 Begins recording his thoughts on art and philosophy in what will become a lifelong practice of reflecting on his art making and the ideas behind it.

Learns to carve wood from Leo Amino, one of his professors at Cooper Union, and starts exploring sculpture.

Meets Mary Staikos, a fellow student at Cooper Union.

Artist Robert Blackburn, whom Whitten meets at Cooper Union, introduces him to Romare Bearden, who in turn introduces him to Jacob Lawrence and Norman Lewis.

Marries Florence Squires.

Moves to 36 Lispenard Street in SoHo.

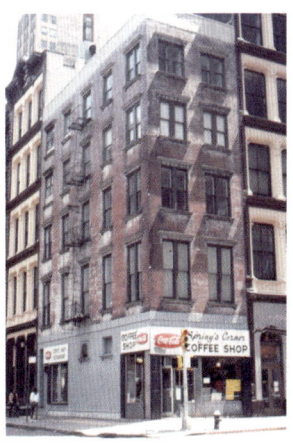

36 Lispenard Street, New York

1964 Whitten's first daughter, Keita, is born. He and Florence divorce shortly after Keita's birth.

Meets Allan Stone, his first art dealer.

Begins his Head paintings, also known as the Ghost paintings (all 1964). These are the first works in which he abandons traditional methods of painting, most notably by working without a brush, instead spreading black and white acrylic paint directly onto the canvas

with a scraper, then placing a thin layer of fabric directly on the still-wet paint and wiping down any excess that seeped through the fabric.

1967 Encouraged by Stone and his artist friends, returns to working with a brush, producing (among other works) his Gardens series (1967–69), a colorful group of abstract paintings in the lineage of Abstract Expressionism.

1968 Marries Mary Staikos.

Meets artists Frank Bowling, Melvin Edwards, Al Loving, and William T. Williams.

His first solo exhibition, *Paintings and Drawings 1967–1968*, opens at Allan Stone Gallery, New York.

1969 Travels with Mary to visit Greece for the first time, going first to Athens, then to Crete, eventually arriving in Agia Galini. They will continue to spend their summers in the village, renting houses until they purchase their own property in 1984. In addition to fishing, Whitten spends these summers focused on making sculpture rather than painting.

1970 Moves away from gestural abstraction and the legacy of Abstract Expressionism and begins exploring new methods of experimenting with paint and tools, including his developers massive wooden rakes he created that move large amounts of paint in single strokes; some were as large as twelve feet wide.

Receives a grant from the Xerox Corporation and begins experimenting with applying toner–which needs only heat to bind to its support–directly to paper and canvas. Demonstrating his interest in finding novel applications for new technologies, he goes on to make several works throughout the 1970s using this approach.

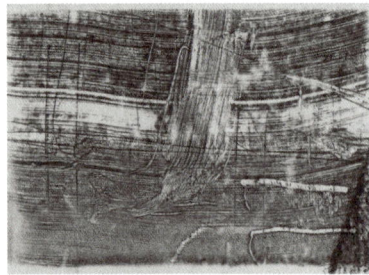

Xerox Project (Flat Plate Monoprint), 1974. Toner on rice paper, 10 × 14½ in. (25.4 × 36.6 cm)

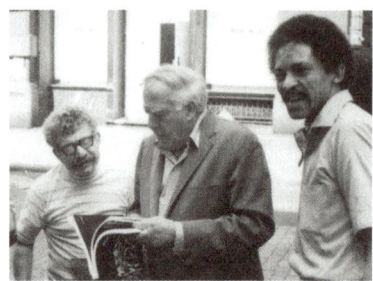

From left: Herman Cherry, Philip Guston, and Whitten, 1972

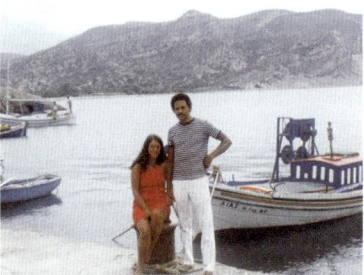

Jack and Mary Whitten in Agia Galini's harbor, Crete, 1971

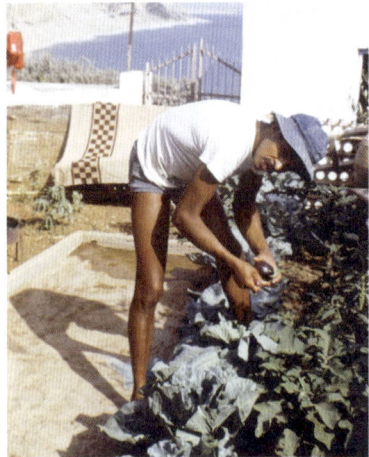

Jack Whitten, Crete, 1972

1972 His second daughter, Mirsini, is born.

Uses the developer to create his first Slab paintings (1972–74).

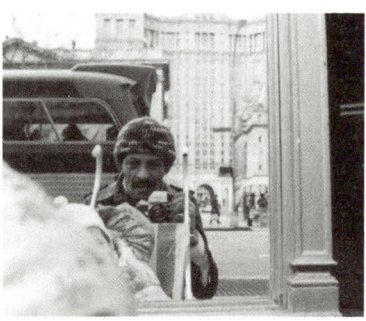

Whitten with his daughter Mirsini, in New York, ca. 1973–74

1974 At the beginning of the year, Marcia Tucker, curator of painting and sculpture at the Whitney Museum of American Art, New York, invites him to have a solo exhibition. *Jack Whitten* opens at the museum that May, featuring twelve paintings.

1975 Begins Greek Alphabet paintings (1975–78).

Henry Geldzahler acquires *Delta Group II* (1975) for the permanent collection of the Metropolitan Museum of Art, New York.

1976 Awarded the Solomon R. Guggenheim Fellowship.

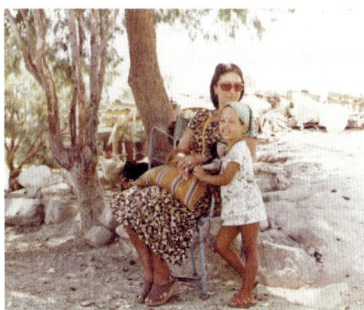

Mary and Mirsini Whitten, Mandres, Crete, 1976

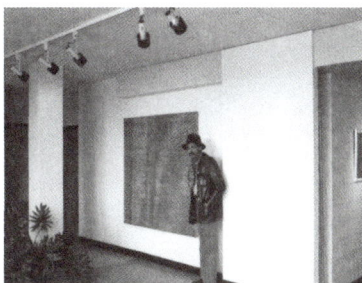

Whitten with *Eta Group III* (1976) in the exhibition *Jack Whitten: Paintings*, Gallery One, Montclair State College, New Jersey, 1977

1978 Kynaston McShine, curator at the Museum of Modern Art, New York, acquires *Kappa I* (1976) for the permanent collection.

1980 Fire destroys his Lispenard Street home and studio, right before he and Mary had planned to buy the building. The damage and subsequent repairs take three years away from his studio practice.

1983 His midcareer retrospective, *Jack Whitten: Ten Years, 1970–1980*, opens at the Studio Museum in Harlem, New York, curated by Henry Geldzahler.

1984 With Mary, buys a hilltop property in Greece, outside of Agia Galini, where they begin building a small home.

Exhibits his sculpture on the beach as part of a festival celebrating the hundredth anniversary of the founding of Agia Galini.

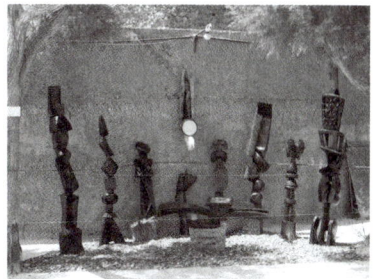

Outdoor exhibition of Whitten's sculpture on the occasion of Agia Galini's hundredth anniversary, 1984

1987 In the summer he and Mary move into their house in Agia Galini while it is still under construction and continue working on it over the next two summers. Whitten does not make sculpture during these summers, focusing instead on building the house.

1988 Begins his seminal *Black Monolith* series with *Black Monolith I, A Tribute to James Baldwin*. Each painting is dedicated to a significant Black historical or cultural figure.

1992 Throughout the 1990s, continues to experiment with acrylic paint and abstraction, increasingly incorporating what he eventually calls tesserae into his work, applying small tiles made from dried acrylic paint directly onto the canvas. This method allows him to experiment with the relationship between light and surface in new ways and further liberates him from traditional painting techniques.

On May 21, *Jack Whitten: Paintings*, the first exhibition of his tesserae paintings, opens at Hordoner-Romley Gallery, New York.

2000 Visits Saint Catherine's Monastery at Sinai on a trip to Egypt and is fascinated by the art and architecture, particularly the mosaics in the basilica. It is after this trip that he begins to conceive of the acrylic blocks he uses as tesserae named after the small stones and tiles used in traditional mosaics.

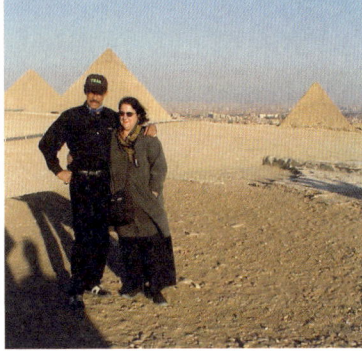

Jack and Mary Whitten at the Great Pyramids, Giza, Egypt, 2000

2001 Travels to Africa and visits the Door of No Return at the House of Slaves Museum and memorial on Gorée Island, off the coast of Dakar, Senegal.

Witnesses the September 11 terrorist attack on the World Trade Center from his studio less than a mile away.

2003 Moves to Queens, New York, in January. In February, finds a two-story former firehouse in Woodside to use as his studio.

2006 Makes his first painting in his new studio, *9.11.01*, dedicated to those who died on September 11.

2007 *Jack Whitten*, a solo exhibition focusing on *9.11.01* as well as his series of Martin Luther King Jr. paintings from the 1960s, opens at MoMA PS1 in Long Island City, Queens.

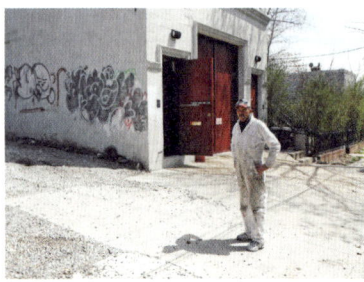

Whitten outside his Woodside, Queens, studio, 2007

2009 In a studio note from March, Whitten writes, "FROM THIS DATE FORWARD MY STUDIO LOG WILL BE KNOWN AS NOTES FROM THE WOODSHED," invoking the term jazz musicians use for practicing in private.

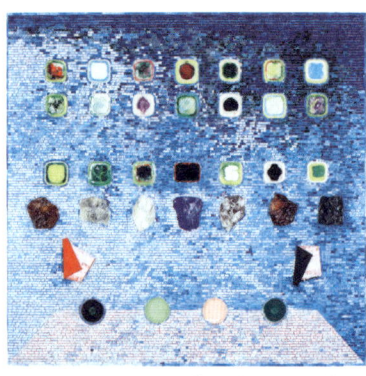

Apps for Obama, 2011. Acrylic on hollow core door, 84 × 91 in. (213.4 × 231.1 cm)

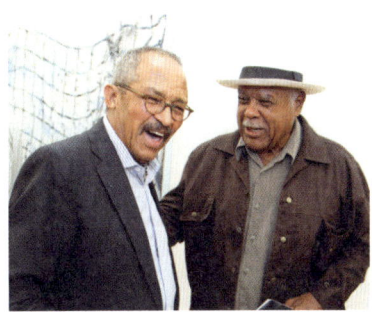

Whitten and Melvin Edwards in front of Whitten's *Crushed Grid* (2013) at the opening of his show at Alexander Gray Associates, New York, 2013

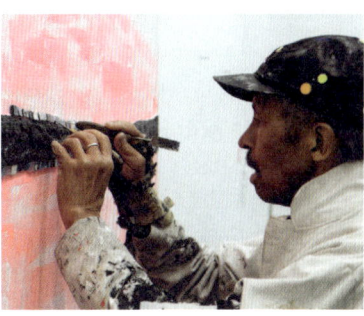

Whitten applying tesserae in his Woodside, Queens, studio to what will be his last painting, *Quantum Wall, VIII (For Arshile Gorky, My First Love in Painting)*, 2018

2014–15 The retrospective *Jack Whitten: Five Decades of Painting* opens at the Museum of Contemporary Art, San Diego, and travels to the Walker Art Center, Minneapolis, and the Wexner Center for the Arts, Columbus, Ohio.

2016 Awarded the 2015 National Medal of Arts by President Barack Obama.

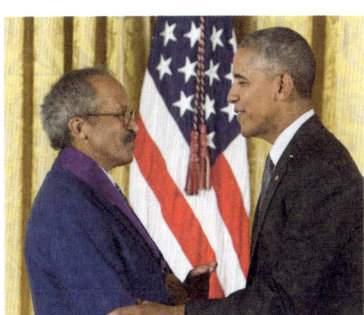

President Barack Obama awarding Whitten the 2015 National Medal of Arts during a ceremony at the White House, Washington, D.C., 2016

2017 Awarded the Skowhegan Medal for Painting.

2018 Whitten dies on January 20 at the age of seventy-eight.

Additional Resources

Particularly in the years since his passing, several significant publications have evaluated Whitten's legacy, unpacking its nuances and impact. Many of these books pull from Whitten's extensive writings, allowing his own voice to shed light on the various complex ideas animating his paintings, sculpture, and works on paper; and their illustrations—from the documentation of his works in the exhibition catalogues and monographs to the facsimiles of his studio notes in his book of writings— illuminate the stunning physicality of his artistic output.

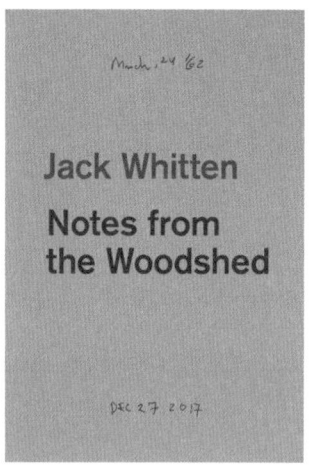

Jack Whitten: Notes from the Woodshed (2018; 2nd ed., 2025) is the authoritative collection of Whitten's writings, presenting the artist's prolific studio notes and other texts spanning from the early 1960s to his death in 2018, accompanied by facsimiles of select documents. Edited by Katy Siegel, the book is now in its second edition, which includes a new afterword in the form of a conversation on Whitten between curators Matilde Guidelli-Guidi and Zoé Whitley and artist Glenn Ligon.

Odyssey: Jack Whitten Sculpture, 1963–2017 (2018) documents the 2018 exhibition of Whitten's sculpture at the Baltimore Museum of Art and Metropolitan Museum of Art, New York. The definitive publication on Whitten's sculptural practice, the book includes essays from Kwame Anthony Appiah, Kelly Baum, Kellie Jones, Richard Shiff, Katy Siegel (who also edited the book), and others; an interview with Whitten by Courtney J. Martin; and a chronology of Whitten's life written by the artist himself.

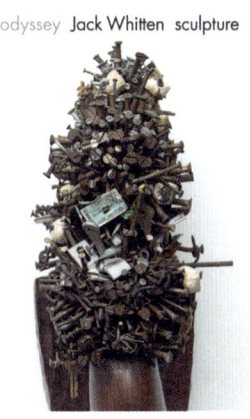

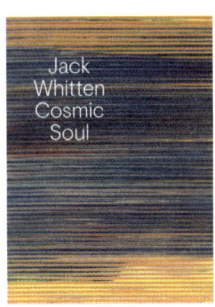

Jack Whitten: Cosmic Soul (2022) gathers several revised and expanded essays as well as new writing by art historian Richard Shiff to offer a multifaceted and critical interpretation of Whitten's artmaking and philosophy of life.

Jack Whitten: The Greek Alphabet Paintings (2023) accompanied the exhibition of this series at Dia Beacon, New York. Painted between 1975 and 1978, the sixty predominantly achromatic compositions demonstrate the artist's conceptual and process-based rigor. The book offers insight on both these works and Whitten's painting overall, with essays by Gregg Bordowitz, Donna De Salvo, Matilde Guidelli-Guidi, Courtney J. Martin, and Fred Moten, alongside previously unpublished archival materials, including selections from Whitten's writings.

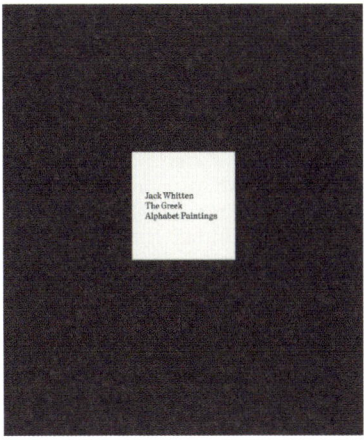

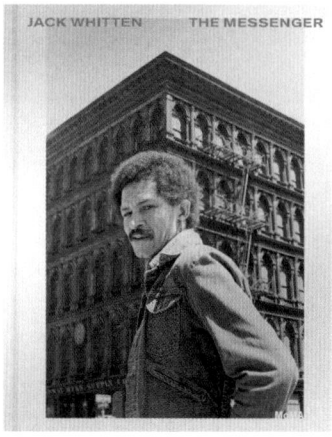

Jack Whitten: The Messenger (2025) was published on the occasion of the first comprehensive retrospective of the artist's work, presented at the Museum of Modern Art, New York. It includes texts by exhibition curator Michelle Kuo; artists Julie Mehretu, Glenn Ligon, and Anna Deavere Smith; art historians Mark Godfrey, Sampada Aranke, Richard Shiff, and others; and groundbreaking technical analyses by the museum's conservators.

Videos of Whitten can be accessed via the code above. They include his wide-ranging discussion about the past, present, and future of painting with art historian Richard Shiff, held on the occasion of the opening of his traveling retrospective *Five Decades of Painting* at the Walker Art Center, Minneapolis; the artist's 2016 lecture "Closing the Gap Between Painting and Sculpture" for the Boston University School of Visual Arts Contemporary Perspectives Lecture Series, in which he articulates the intersections between developments in his artistic practice and philosophy; and Art21's "Jack Whitten: An Artist's Life" (2018), from the *Extended Play* series, which features footage of Whitten in the studio using his tesserae to make what would become his final painting, *Quantum Wall, VIII (For Arshile Gorky, My First Love in Painting)* (2017).

Sources

Most quotations from the artist are from *Jack Whitten: Notes from the Woodshed* (New York: Hauser & Wirth Publishers, 2018; 2nd ed., 2025), cited below as *Notes*.

p. 9: Quote from Whitten's January 22, 1986, entry in *Notes*, p. 185.

pp. 19–20: Whitten's quotations about "subjective images" and "the development of a new esthetic" are from his January 26–31, 1973, entry in *Notes*, pp. 43–44.

p. 21: "I see no paintings to excite me..." is from Whitten's January 26–31, 1973, entry in *Notes*, p. 46.

p. 23: "I've done so much..." is from Whitten's October 1972, entry in *Notes*, p. 41.

p. 24: "I wanted this slab to be a concrete fact..." is from "Fourth and Fifth Testing (Slab)," 2014, unpublished typescript, cited in Richard Shiff, *Cosmic Soul* (New York: Hauser & Wirth Publishers, 2022), pp. 46–47.

p. 33: "About midway through the service..." is from Whitten in conversation with Jarrett Earnest, *Brooklyn Rail*, February 2017, https://brooklynrail.org/2017/02/art/JACK-WHITTEN-with-Jarrett-Earnest/.

p. 34: "My use of acrylic tesserae is a unit..." is from Whitten's October 6, 2012, entry in *Notes*, p. 457.

p. 35: "The painting is somatic..." is from Whitten's undated notes cited in *Jack's Jacks* (Munich: Prestel, 2019), p. 152.

p. 54: "I actually handled his stuff" and "had a revelation during an early morning ROTC class..." are from Whitten, "Chronology," in *Odyssey: Jack Whitten Sculpture, 1963-2017* (New York: Gregory R. Miller; Baltimore: Baltimore Museum of Art, 2018), pp. 176 and 177.

p. 60: "If there was ever a lesson for me..." is from Melvin Edwards in "Melvin Edwards and Senior Curator Katy Siegel on Jack Whitten's Artistic Legacy," June 12, 2018, Baltimore Museum of Art, cited in Shiff, *Cosmic Soul*, p. 281.

p. 62: "I wasn't really interested in Abstract Expressionism..." is from William T. Williams in "An Oral History with William T. Williams by Mona Hadler," *BOMB*, February 19, 2018, https://bombmagazine.org/articles/2018/02/19/william-t-williams-by-mona-hadler/.

p. 64: "I miss Harvey..." and other quotations about Quaytman and the painting Whitten dedicated to him are from Whitten's December 27, 2008, entry in *Notes*, p. 379.

p. 66: "Here is a man..." is from Whitten in conversation with Andrianna Campbell (2015) in *Notes*, p. 535.

p. 71: "I give thanks to God..." is from Whitten's January 31, 1963, entry in *Notes*, p. 168.

p. 72: "The painting 9.11.01..." is from Whitten's April 3, 2006, entry in *Notes*, p. 332.

pp. 81–82: Whitten mentions "formal sensations," Allan Stone's instructions for interacting with African objects, and "elemental matter" in Whitten, "Why Do I Carve Wood?" (2017) in *Odyssey*, pp. 37–39.

p. 84: "Extraordinary journey in three dimensions..." is from Roberta Smith, "Revealing a Secret Art Life: A Painter's Sculptures," *New York Times*, September 6, 2018, https://www.nytimes.com/2018/09/06/arts/design/jack-whitten-review-met-breuer-sculpture.html.

p. 87: "I saw a tree standing in a clearing..." is from Whitten in conversation with Courtney J. Martin, *Odyssey*, p. 147.

p. 93: "I have been carving wood..." is from Whitten's November 29, 2012, entry in *Notes*, p. 467.

p. 104: "Objects do not exist..." is from Whitten's March 24, 1962, entry in *Notes*, p. 26. "Beneath every surface..." is from June 24, 1964, *Notes*, pp. 35–36. "I have made a full circle..." is from February 18, 1973, p. 50. "The trip to California..." is from March 25, 1973, p. 51. "I DID NOT GET THE GUGGENHEIM..." is from March 25, 1974, p. 69.

p. 105: "I have been so depressed..." is from Whitten's March 25, 1974, entry in *Notes*, p. 72. "Today I am forty years old..." is from December 5, 1979, p. 159.

pp. 106–15: Whitten's "Battle Plan" and "Objectives" appear in *Notes* on pp. 171–76 and pp. 302–4, respectively.

p. 117: "THE DUKE WENT OUT TODAY..." is from Whitten's May 24, 1974, entry in *Notes*, p. 81.

p. 119: "Molecular perception is the key..." is from Whitten's March 31, 2017, entry in *Notes*, pp. 577–78.

pp. 119–20: "Style is a bad word for me..." is from Whitten in conversation with Charlie Finch, "Art Breaking," WBAI, 1994, radio program.

p. 122: "A great opportunity..." is from Whitten's September 28, 2012, entry in *Notes*, p. 256.

pp. 122–24: "Five Lines Four Spaces" was originally published in *Blues for Smoke* (Los Angeles: Museum of Contemporary Art; New York: DelMonico Books/Prestel, 2012), pp. 148–49. It also appears in *Notes*, pp. 462–64.

p. 129: "Putting words into the feelings..." from Whitten in Whitten and Stacie Lindner, "About the Subjects," in Stuart Horodner and Lindner, *Jack Whitten: Memorial Paintings* (Atlanta: Atlanta Contemporary Art Center, 2008), p. 53.

p. 130: "Just viewing it is so impressive..." is from Whitten in Judith Olch Richards, "Oral History with Jack Whitten, 2009, December 1–3," Archives of American Art, Smithsonian Institution, https://www.aaa.si.edu /collections/ interviews/oral-history-interview -jackwhitten- 15748. "I could spend the rest of my life..." is from Whitten, "*Black Monolith X (The Birth of Muhammad Ali)*," November 2016, unpublished note, cited in "The Black Monoliths" in *Odyssey*, p. 112.

p. 152: "FROM THIS DATE FORWARD..." is from Whitten's March 1, 2009, entry in *Notes*, p. 385.

Additional Captions

Cover: Jack Whitten with *Pink Psyche Queen* (1973), ca. 1975

pp. 4–5: Whitten in his Crosby Street studio, New York, ca. 1974–75

pp. 7–6: Whitten's Lispenard Street studio, New York, ca. late 1960s

pp. 8–9: Whitten carving wood, Agia Galini, Crete, 1986

pp. 10–11: Whitten's Lispenard Street studio, New York, 1988

pp. 12–13: Whitten's Woodside studio, 2019

pp. 14–15: *The Afro American Thunderbolt*, 1983–84. Black mulberry, copper plate, nails, 10 × 8 × 24 in. (25.4 × 20.3 × 61 cm)

p. 160: Paintbrushes in Whitten's Woodside studio, 2019

Credits

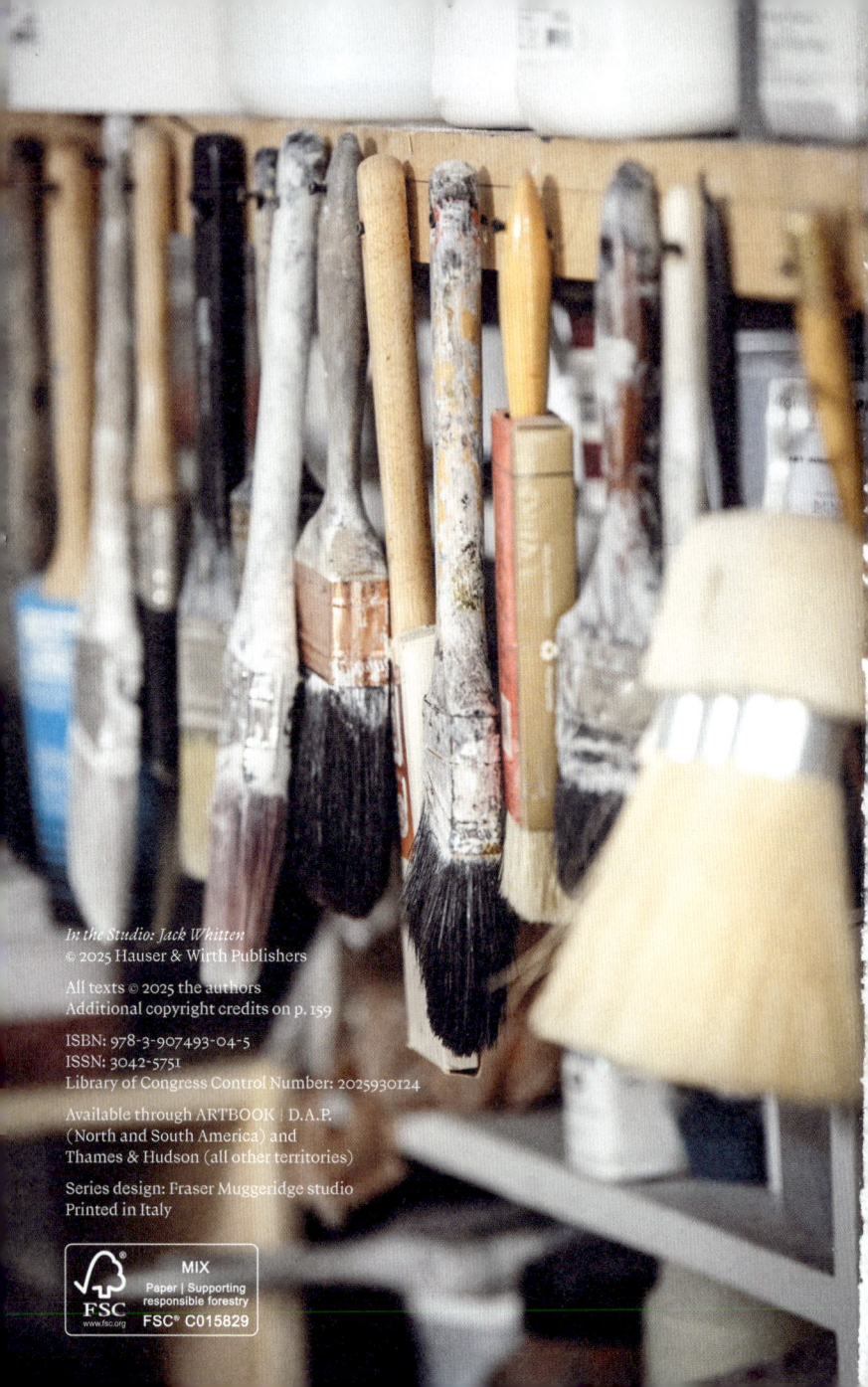

In the Studio: Jack Whitten
© 2025 Hauser & Wirth Publishers

All texts © 2025 the authors
Additional copyright credits on p. 159

ISBN: 978-3-907493-04-5
ISSN: 3042-5751
Library of Congress Control Number: 2025930124

Available through ARTBOOK | D.A.P.
(North and South America) and
Thames & Hudson (all other territories)

Series design: Fraser Muggeridge studio
Printed in Italy